THE RIVER JORDAN

A True Story of the Underground Railroad

Henry Burke & Dick Croy

a *Watershed* Book
Marietta, Ohio

THE RIVER JORDAN
A True Story of the Underground Railroad

By Henry Burke & Dick Croy

Published by Watershed Books
130 Warner St.
Marietta, OH 45750
www.watershedbooks.com
publisher@watershedbooks.com

Printed in Canada

Refuge for runaway slaves

Copyright © 2001

10 9 8 7 6 5 4 3

Publisher's Cataloging-in-Publication
(Provided by Quality Books, Inc.)

Burke, Henry Robert, 1940-
 The River Jordan : a true story of the underground railroad / Henry Burke & Dick Croy. -- 1st ed.
 p. cm.
 LCCN 2001-131406
 ISBN 0-9645252-2-4

 1. Underground railroad--Fiction. 2. Fugitive slaves --United States--History--19th century--Fiction. 3. United States--History--Civil War, 1861-1865-- Afro-Americans--Fiction. 4. Ohio--History--Civil War, 1861-1865--Fiction. I. Croy, Dick. II. Title.

PS3503.U6125R58 2001   813'.54
                    QB101-700179

This book is dedicated to the slaves who helped build America and to those who risked their lives, their livelihoods, the safety of their families to set them free.

Escape of Slaves.

On Sunday night last, eleven slaves escaped from Virginia, and reached Marietta about daylight on Monday morning. Ten of the number were from the plantation of Mr. S. Harness, who resides about seven miles above this place. It is supposed that in the fog of the night they lost their way, and missed the point where they intended to land, and where they probably expected aid to remove themselves and their baggage to a place of safety.

Be this as it may, at day light they were here, and were compelled to leave their goods and flee. In a couple of hours Mr. Harness, and others arrived in pursuit. Two of the fugitives were, in the course of the day, found in a barn near the river, but all efforts to discover the others have thus far been in vain. They are probably many miles from here—far out of the reach of their pursuers.

The two discovered, were taken before Esq., Buell for examination. Application was soon made to Judge Cotton for a writ of Habeus Corpus, which was issued, and in obedience to the command of which, Mr. Harness appeared with the slaves, to show why he detained them.—Arius Nye Esq. appeared as counsel for Mr. Harness, and W. D. Emerson & Jno. Wilson Esqrs., for the slaves. After the examination of several witnesses, the council in behalf of the slaves admitted that there was no legal objection to the return of the fugitives to their master, and thereupon his Honor dismissed the writ. They were again taken before Esq. Buell, to whom application was made for a certificate directing their return to Mr. Harness, and authorizing him to remove them back to Virginia. This certificate was granted, and the slaves delivered to Mr. H. who immediately removed them home.

There was manifest, during the entire proceedings, a feeling of great sympathy for the slaves, and but few could be induced by the large offers of reward to engage in pursuing or hunting them out.

$450 REWARD

RANAWAY from the subscriber, living in *Wood County* in the state of *Virginia*, EIGHT Negro Slaves, to wit: .

JANE, a woman of low stature and very fleshy, and abou fifty years of age, something lame in one leg when walking.

ALFRED, a young man of about *twenty five years o* age, spare made, has a remarkable hole in his left jaw, & plays on the Violi Caroline, a heavy built young woman. aged about **23**, copper coloured, na has a scar about one of her eyes, and some freckles. Rachael, a sma spare built woman. quite black, about **22** years of age, with remarkab prominent eyes. Augustus, a heavy stout built boy about **16** years old, qui black, and marked on one of his arms under his sleeve with a honey com and plays well on the Violin. Thornton, a boy about **14** years of age, st built, and very bushy headed. Henry, **12** or **13** years old, a handsome rather slender, very black. Fanny, about **8** or **9** years old, has ba burn upon her wrist, leaving a scar differing in color from her skin.

For Alfred I will pay **$100**; for one and each of the oth named slaves, I will give **$50** each if delivered to me at m residence, in Wood Co. Va. at the mouth of Bull Creek.

S. HARNESS.

Wood Co, Va., Aug. **21**, 1843

INTRODUCTION

To me the subject of the Underground Railroad is very personal. It is the greatest story of freedom in American history and I feel it in my soul. The history of the Underground Railroad also involved my family's rise from slavery and their fight to free other African-Americans in the Civil War.

As a child, I developed a great interest in where my family had originated and how they'd come to southeastern Ohio. I didn't learn about the Underground Railroad in a classroom. I learned about the Freedom Trail from my relatives and many others who, like me, cherished the tradition that our ancestors had contributed to the freedom of African-American people in our country. I have spent nearly all my life developing a perspective about the Underground Railroad along the Ohio River, while researching my family's origins in Virginia.

Ancestors of the Burke family were brought from Africa to the Corotoman Plantation in Lancaster County, Virginia, by John Carter as early as 1640, about the time the plantation was founded. Some Burke ancestors may even have been on the first ship to Virginia in 1619. In any case, my family's ancestors were among the earliest Africans brought into the English Colonies of North America.

Robert King Carter (1663-1736), the son of Col. John Carter, became America's first millionaire. He owned over a thousand slaves and held almost 300,000 acres of plantation land in the northern neck of Virginia. His land holdings included the famous Carter Grove Plantation, now a part of the United States Park Service at Williamsburg, Virginia. Descendants of the original Carters included American presidents Benjamin and

William Henry Harrison and Robert E. Lee, father of the Confederacy.

Robert King Carter's son Robert Carter Jr. (1704-1732) died very young, leaving a four-year-old son of his own. Robert Carter, III, (1728-1804) inherited a large number of slaves and an estate that included some 78,000 acres. He eventually established a plantation on Nomini Creek in Westmoreland County, Virginia, near the present-day city of Montross. Around 1791 he freed nearly 500 of his slaves, the largest emancipation by an individual slaveholder in the history of the United States.

Among those freed was my ancestor Winny Burke, whose son Joseph brought his family to Washington County in 1854. When the Civil War broke out, Joseph's son Nimrod was hired as a civilian teamster and scout by Lieutenant Colonel Melvin C. Clark, a prominent Marietta, Ohio, attorney who had employed Nimrod before the war. In March, 1864, after President Lincoln opened the way for the Union Army to enlist free blacks and emancipated slaves, Nimrod became a sergeant with the 23rd U.S. Colored Infantry Regiment. The 23rd participated in the fall of Petersburg in April, 1865, and pursued Lee's forces to Appomattox, where on April 9 Lee surrendered to end the Civil War. Thus had slavery come full circle in the history of my family. Carter descendant Robert E. Lee lay down his arms to victorious Union forces which included my great-great-grandfather Nimrod Burke, whose ancestors had helped make the Carter family the richest and most powerful in America.

To understand what motivated African-Americans to run from slavery, one needs only to ask a few basic questions: Who were the slaves? How had they become slaves? What perpetuated slavery? What would my life be like if I were a slave myself?

These are the questions that prompted my own fascination with the Underground Railroad, which goes back to my earliest memories. My grandparents John (1889-1967) and Anna (Curtis) Burke (1888-1973) raised me in their home in Marietta, Ohio, in Washington County. My early lessons about the Underground

Railroad came from my grandmother's family and the village of Stafford in Monroe County, where she was born and raised. Stafford was an abolitionist center with a very busy station on the Underground Railroad.

My grandmother Anna was the daughter of Cisley Curtis and granddaughter of "Rockingham" John Curtis (1830-1914), born on a plantation in Rockingham County, Virginia. Rockingham John was a legendary ancestor about whom I've written extensively. Due to Cisley's death soon after giving birth to my grandmother, John Curtis raised Anna as his own child. He also had another daughter, Laura, and six sons. Both daughters and one son had long been dead when I came along, but five sons – Tom, Clem, Ike, Ed and John Henry – were still alive during the 1940s when I was young. Clem, Ike and Ed all lived near Stafford, where my grandmother and I spent nearly every weekend and where, from the age of five, I spent every day of my summer vacation with my great-uncle Ed Curtis. I was very fond of a big ancient gray workhorse named Harry. Though at first I had difficulty getting on Old Harry, as I called him, I soon learned to maneuver him to a place where I could climb aboard; then I would ride him up and down the road, pretending to be my great-great-grandfather Rockingham John.

It was during these visits that I became aware of Underground Railroad trails leading northward to Stafford from the Ohio River. I thought that the Underground Railroad began and ended near Stafford; I had no real concept of slavery although I had heard it discussed. I knew that Rockingham John had been a slave. He had worked with the Stafford Underground Railroad, and the stories of his many exploits were told over and over – the most vivid during our winter weekend visits around a big fireplace in a cabin shared by Clem and Ed. There was no electricity and since lamp oil was considered expensive even it was used sparingly, so the fireplace provided light as well as heat. This was such a special time, when the oral history of the Underground Railroad was passed down to me.

Then when I was eleven years old, tragedy struck. As usual, I had gone to Stafford to stay with my uncle Ed for the summer. He had mowed and raked some hay in a field above the house, and we loaded the hay wagon, which was hitched to an inexperienced new horse. Uncle Ed and I were sitting on top of the load. On the way to the barn, the young horse ran off. Although I managed to jump from the back of the wagon, receiving only minor injuries, Uncle Ed fell behind the runaway horse and became entangled in the traces. Critically injured, he was taken by a neighbor to the hospital in Marietta, where he died a few hours later. My visits to Stafford and my childhood ended that afternoon.

I was lost back in Marietta. I just couldn't cope with the loss of Uncle Ed. Nothing interested me. I was in a daze that made it impossible for me to concentrate. I had spent every hour of every summer of my life in Stafford with Uncle Ed. Today such a condition would probably be recognized as Post Traumatic Stress Syndrome. In 1951, we just called it "feeling low." This was when I first realized that death was final. Before the accident, I had more or less believed that everything would go on unchanged forever.

I finally decided to run away from home, for the first and only time in my life. (I'm still not sure how serious I really was.) The whole episode lasted only about ten hours and covered about twenty miles round-trip. Though geographically I didn't travel far, in a psychological sense, my trip took me to the other side of the universe.

For some weeks, I had lived in an imaginary realm where time stood still and nothing ever changed. I was a listless spirit, wandering through an empty void; a mute observer to a horrendous tragedy, unable to change or control anything. My poor grandmother, enduring her own grief, finally bought me a horse to console me. I kept him at the Washington County Fairgrounds, just a couple of blocks from where we lived in Marietta.

Early one August morning, I saddled Dan and rode him through town and across the Ohio River to Williamstown, West Virginia, then headed north on the old Waverly Pike. It soon grew very hot as we plodded upstream along the Ohio, but I was determined to put distance between myself and the sadness at home.

Around 10 a.m. I was thirsty enough to stop at a house and ask for a drink of water. A warm-hearted lady working in her garden gave me a glass of lemonade instead, and I continued on with renewed vigor. Sometime before noon, I reached Bull Creek at the north end of the little town of Waverly. I was only about ten miles from home, but Dan was sweating badly from the heat radiating off the asphalt pavement.

After crossing the bridge over Bull Creek, Dan climbed a long gentle grade and I was soon thirsty again. The thought of giving up had begun to creep into my mind. Then just ahead on the right, I spotted an old man sitting on a bench in the shade of an oak tree in front of a big old farmhouse. I noticed that he had a funny little cap cocked sideways on his head. That dingy, sweat-stained gray cap turned out to be of Civil War vintage.

I stopped and exchanged greetings with the old man, whose name was Bill Harness, then got directly to the point. He directed me to a well at the side of the house. The pump had a crank, with an old tin cup hanging on a hook on the faucet. There was a three-gallon bucket sitting nearby. I turned the crank and filled the bucket for Dan, then took the tin cup and drank deeply. I can't remember a time when water tasted any better. What a pleasant relief the shade of that grand old oak tree gave me! I just took my time.

When Dan and I had finally finished drinking, I replaced the tin cup and bucket and thanked Bill Harness again for the water.

"Sit a spell and rest yer hoss," he said after looking Dan over. I gladly accepted the offer and tied Dan to the tree. "Nice hoss yer got there."

We just sat there on the bench in the shade, gazing out at the two-lane blacktop. Occasionally a car or truck would roll by, but traffic was light in this part of the country back in 1951.

Finally Bill asked in his hillbilly twang, "Whar yer headed?"

"Pittsburgh I reckon."

"Whoa, ah reckon yer got you a fur piece ta go, don' cha?"

"Yup." I had no idea how far away Pittsburgh was; I wasn't even sure I was headed in the right direction. For something to say, I offered, "Nice place ya got here."

"It'll do till something better comes along," he said with a big grin. Then he asked bluntly, "What ta hell you agoin' all the way to Pittsburgh fer?"

"To git a job I guess," was the best answer I could come up with.

"Yer Ma know whar yer agoin'?"

"Sure thing," I lied.

"Hmmm," he said.

We continued to sit for a while, then Bill asked, "What's yer name agi'n?"

I told him.

"I was jest thinkin' yer might be some kin to them there slaves mah gran'pappy Solomon Harness used t' keep 'round cher."

...I heard what the man said, but my mind wasn't responding. In the first place, I still didn't understand the historic issues about slavery very well. It had certainly never crossed my mind that slaves had been kept right across the Ohio River.

He went on to tell me a long story about slaves and slavery in West Virginia, the northern-most part of Virginia until 1863. As Bill saw it, slavery had darn near ruined his family. Because they had slaves to do their work, he said, a whole generation of the Harness family had become complacent.

We talked for some time before I noticed that the sun had moved a considerable distance toward the west. Bill realized it too. "Yer best be headin' back if yer wanna make home afore dark."

"See ya later," I told him, climbing back on Dan. It was a little cooler now, and old Dan stretched into a long ground-covering shuffle. We arrived in Marietta a lot faster than we'd reached Bull Creek. It wasn't quite dark when I finally took Dan to the stable, watered and fed him, then walked the two blocks home. My mother, who was home from work, assumed I'd spent the day at the Fairgrounds as usual.

After that first conversation with Bill Harness, I unconsciously began to file away every little bit of information I could find about slavery in the Mid-Ohio Valley. Over the years

I went to see Bill quite a few times. The last time, before joining the Army in the fall of '58, he showed me a tumbled-down old cabin sitting between the highway and the Ohio River. Bill said it had been built clear back in 1790 by an early settler who purchased the land from George Washington.

He told me many stories about events around Bull Creek before it became part of West Virginia. I always kept them in mind; they broadened my interest in the enslavement of African-American people and the Underground Railroad that set so many of them free.

When I returned to Marietta in 1967 after nine years' military service, I found employment as a heavy equipment operator in surface coal mines and on projects building highways and electric power plants. For thirty years I worked on many construction projects extending along the Ohio River from Wheeling downriver to Huntington, West Virginia. In every place I worked along the Ohio, someone would tell me a story about slavery and the Underground Railroad.

Around 1980, I became acquainted with Louise Zimmer and Jerry Devol, local experts on Washington County history. I discussed my research with them on a regular basis as I continued to study the Underground Railroad as a serious hobby. So many people have contributed information to my research over the years that I can't possibly remember all of them, but a list of those who have helped most significantly appears on the Acknowledgments Page.

In 1985, my co-author Dick Croy returned to Marietta to take over his family's business, and our paths crossed a year or so later when he called me for information concerning a book he was writing. When I told him of the many stories about the Underground Railroad that I'd been collecting and writing down, he was quite interested and asked to see some of them. That began a collaboration which, over more than a decade, has led to the book you're about to read as well as a number of other projects. *The River Jordan* began as a short story entitled "The Escape of Jane" and just kept growing.

I have now spent many years researching my family's heritage, which I feel is an extraordinary story within the framework of African-American history. An unbounded curiosity was first aroused by names and voices from another century, in front of a huge stone fireplace in an old cabin on a former Underground Railroad route in southeastern Ohio. A solidly built cabin erected near Stafford in 1866 by my great-great-grandfather, former slave Rockingham John Curtis.

Henry Robert Burke
February, 2001

ACKNOWLEDGMENTS

The authors would like to thank the following people for their invaluable contributions and encouragement: Charles Fogle for the excellent maps within and supplementary to the book, Christina Ullman for the evocative cover, and Sandra Moats for information about western Virginia abolitionists. Thanks to the following who read early drafts of the ms.: Dr. Ancella Bickley for a detailed critical assessment, correspondence in behalf of the project, and the descriptive paragraph on the back cover; Bennie McCrae <http://www.coax.net/people/lwf/default.htm> for his abiding interest in Mr. Burke's many years of URR research and for hosting his Website: www.coax.net/people/lwf/hrb_seo.htm; Nancy Hoy and Ruth Thorniley for historical and architectural information; Rebecca Bennett, Joy Croy, Patsy Evans, Robert Hinton, John Mattox, John Ogden, Dr. Lorle Porter, Cathe Poulson (a strong supporter when the authors really needed one), David Prather, Susan Sheppard, Jerry Vance and Louise Zimmer for their helpful comments. Also, Lila Hill; Ben Bain; Richard Walker, Ph.D.; Ernie Thode; Roger Young; Michel Perdreau <http://www.seorf.ohiou.edu/~xxo57>; Mrs. Fred Dickerson; Peggy Neel; Webmaster Mike Shaffer; Michael Stolkey and the people at Fidlar Doubleday.

By Henry Burke & Dick Croy

To native Americans who knew it before the coming of the white man, the wide river was the Oyo-peck-han-ne, or "very white river," from its appearance when ruffled by the region's prevailing southwesterly winds. Later the French under La Salle translated "Oyo" into La Belle Riviere, "the beautiful river." The British, who wrested the vast fertile watershed from the French, knew the Ohio by its Indian name; and with a minor revision in spelling the river has borne it ever since. But in the half century leading up to the Civil War, the waterway separating western Virginia and Kentucky from Ohio, Indiana and Illinois was given biblical stature by those seeking to cross it to secure their freedom from slavery. Comparing themselves to the Israelites fleeing Egypt some 3,000 years earlier, fugitive slaves reverently referred to the natural boundary between slave and free states as *the River Jordan*.

The story you are about to read is a fictionalized account of an actual escape in August, 1843, of the slave Jane and her seven children from a western Virginia tobacco plantation on land once owned by George Washington. All the major characters and events are real, portrayed as reported in newspapers and historical documents of the time. Some minor characters and incidents are authentic as well, while others are fictional characterizations intended to illustrate .and add detail to the historical setting – particularly the operation of the Underground Railroad – in Ohio, from Washington County to Lake Erie, in the mid-1800s.

Among the pertinent newspaper articles of the period is a story headlined "Escape of Slaves" – in the August 24, 1843, edition of the *Marietta Intelligencer* – about the escape across the Ohio River and the capture and court appearance of two of the slaves who accompanied Jane's family. Another artifact is a yellowed copy of the $450 reward poster that slave master Solomon Harness had printed. It describes Jane as "a woman of low stature and very fleshy, and about fifty years of age, something lame in one leg when walking." Harness's contemptuous description of this courageous mother of seven serves only to underscore the heroic journey she undertook to save her family. Yet it was but one among thousands of such stories of heroism and compassion, by black and white Americans alike, on the Underground Railroad.

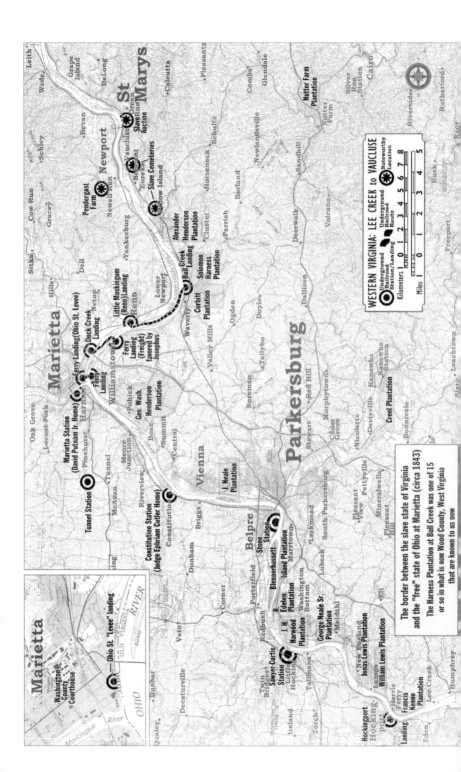

Marietta

Washington County Courthouse

Ohio St. "levee" landing

OLD VIRGINIA

OHIO

RIVER

Muskingum River

Hocking River

WESTERN VIRGINIA: LEE CREEK to VAUCLUSE

- Underground Railroad Station/Landing
- Underground Railroad Route
- ⊛ Noteworthy Location

Kilometers 0 1 2 3 4 5 6 7 8

Miles 0 1 2 3 4 5

The border between the slave state of Virginia and the "free" state of Ohio at Marietta (circa 1843) or so in what is now Wood County, West Virginia that are known to us now

The Harness Plantation at Bull Creek was one of 15

St Marys

Green Slave/Run Auction

Vaucluse Point Eureka

Pendergast Farm

Newell Run

Slave Cemeteries

Cow Island

Newport

Leith

Wade

Grape Island

DeLong

Schley

Bevan

Calcutta

Pleasants

Sitka

Cow Run

Gracey

Dell

Yankeeburg

Netop

Lower Newport

Combs

Glendale

Newlandsville

Schultz

Horseneck

Cluster

Parrish

Silver Run Station

Cairo

Rutherford

Riverside

Racy

Rush

Leachtown

Freeport

Volcano

Doyle

Borland

Sandhill

Deerwalk

Dallison

Ogden

Waverly

Valley Mills

Boreman

Tallyho

Red Hill

Stewart

Murphytown

Kanawha Station

Parkersburg

Bull Creek Landing

Solomon Harness Plantation

Alexander Henderson Plantation

Little Muskingum (Reno) Landing

Reno

Corbitt Plantation

Nutter Farm Plantation

Nutter Farm

Duck Creek Landing

Ferry Landing (Ohio St. Levee)

Ferry Landing (freight) favored by Josephus

Ferry Landing

Marietta

Harmar

Williamstown

Pohick

Boaz

Summit

Central

Marietta Station (David Putnam Jr. Home)

Pinehurst

Moore Junction

Geo. Wash. Henderson Plantation

Vienna

J. Neale Plantation

Riverview

Briggs

Dunham

Corner

Porterfield

Tunnel Station

Tunnel

McAvan

Constitution Station (Judge Ephriam Cutler Home)

Constitution

Oak Grove

Locust Fork

Qualey

Dunbar

Decaturville

Veto

Redbush

Ireland

Torch

Eden

Lee Creek

Humphrey

Francis Keene Plantation

Hockingport Hocking

Harris Landing

New England Jonas Lewis Plantation

William Lewis Plantation

Lamps

George Neale Sr. Plantation

Meldahl

J. H. Harwood Plantation

Sawyer-Curtis Station

Twin Bridges

Little Hocking

Taylmons

Belpre

Stone Station

Blennerhassett

Eden R. Island Plantation

Washington Bottom

Marrtown

Larkmead

Lubeck

South Parkersburg

Eli

Pleasant View

Minerawells

Pettyville

Pleasant Hill

Bonnivale

Nicolette

Davisville

Cedar Grove

Slate

Creel Plantation

1

Jane told herself stand up now, woman, because after 12 hours and a lifetime of pickin', doesn't much matter if it's corn or cotton or tobacco, a body's back is no more ready to straighten itself out come evening than it looked forward to bowing to cold wet tobacco leaves in the foggy damp of first light. Not on Solomon Harness's plantation, his overseer Jeb Porter scowling down all day from that ill-tempered roan stallion of his. Hard eyes hidden always in the shadow of his hat brim so you never know for sure who he's watching, you or one of your own or no one, half asleep in the saddle, blacksnake whip coiled in his right hand, shotgun snug in its leather sling against the saddle. Jane said stand up, woman, that August sun's done had its day and its way again. Time to get the kettle on, get these folks fed before chores. Tonight's got to look like any other night.

She stood up stiffly, driving the pain from its indolent curled-up slumber in her lower back as she did every evening in the transition from field slave to mother. Looking out over the gently rolling fields contoured with undulant rows of ripe tobacco, Jane took command of them, possessed them for a moment the way her children belonged to her, as one honors one's work and the harvest, the fruition and fullness of nature. Maternal power was what made life bearable for this heavy-set woman shielding her eyes from the westering sun, weariness, strength and dignity all apparent in her face and bearing. Her children were the meaning in a life of inexplicable servitude. Every word and action were based on an awareness that whatever fragile hope they had for a better life depended largely on her.

The slight, beautiful young woman with large dark eyes kneeling in the row beside her is Rachel, 22. Harness had been offered a handsome price for Rachel, but Jane was able to persuade his wife Emily to intervene. "He's agreed not to sell her this time, Jane," Emily had said, "but you can't expect to keep her here forever."

Scattered around the two of them, from the drying sheds clear to the river, well over 100 acres in tobacco alone, some 40 or 50 men, women and children work wordlessly at much the same pace: well-oiled components of plantation machinery. Mostly adults split the stalks, cutting them off at the ground, the lank green tobacco leaves made supple and flaccid by the Ohio Valley's humidity and late-summer sun. Younger children carry armfuls of the stalks to their older siblings to load on wagons pulled by teams of somnolent mules.

The somber little girl lugging that wooden bucket of drinking water between rows is Jane's 9-year-old daughter Fanny. Those are her brothers, Henry, 12, and Thornton, 14, laying bundles of tobacco leaves on the wagon bed. Henry's the compact, muscular boy, Thornton the more lithe and graceful of the two.

"Sho be glad when *dis* day over," says Henry under his breath since conversation between slaves in Harness's fields is strictly forbidden.

"Gonna drink dat ole well dry," replies Thornton.

"Don' be talkin' 'bout no water," grumbles Henry. "Tryin' not t' think 'bout it."

"Not thinkin' 'bout how *good* it'd taste? Runnin' all cool an' wet down yo dusty throat?"

"Shut up, Thornton!"

That big strapping, well-favored man driving the wagon just now entering the drying shed is Jane's eldest son Alfred, 25. It's a little cooler in here out of the sun, in the pungent smell of tobacco leaves curing. Hanging the split stalks from those poles running the width of the shed is Caroline, 23, broad-shouldered and big-boned like her daddy. The last time she laid eyes on him she was seven and he was being led in chains up the gangplank of a sternwheeler docked right here at the plantation. Caroline looks a bit peaked. Let's hope it's just fatigue; there's no doctor or infirmary on the Harness plantation. The various herbal remedies Jane's mother Hannah passed on to her might help, but Caroline wouldn't get much respite from her work, no matter how sick she was.

"Massa say, 'Nigger don' make no money for me lyin' 'round all day,'" Jane will tell you. Though she's argued with him enough on behalf of her children, it's never done more than buy them a day's rest now and then after a serious injury or illness.

That's Augustus, 16, talking to Alfred now. A big rough boy who'd almost rather tussle than eat, Augustus can take all the boys his own age to the ground and many older ones too. He's been doing a man's work since the age of 12 and has often told his mother he wants to be a riverboat hand, but Jane's always cut him short lest Master Harness get wind of the notion. Best not to let Harness get the Ohio River and one of her boys in his head at one and the same time.

"Thought you'd never get here," Augustus chides his brother. "Jeb Porter say we cain't quit till this whole wagonload hung."

"Jeb Porter's who I'd like to hang up t' cure. Maybe

- 3 -

mellow some a the meanness out of 'im."

Augustus gestures anxiously for Alfred to shut up as Jeb rides up behind him. "Cut the jawin' and git this wagon onloaded! 'Fore you niggers eat tonight, I want ever' bit a this tobaccy hung, hear me?"

"Yass-suh," reply the brothers in unison. Though Augustus's tone of voice carries the note of subservience called for, Alfred's as usual is deep and impassive. He neither looks at Porter nor looks away.

"Henry!" Jane calls to her youngest son, "Time t' fix supper! Git some kindlin' an' start de fire! Fanny, fetch me some water fo de kettle, chile!"

"You always gets to make de fire," complains Thornton.

"'Cause I makes it de best," Henry taunts him over his shoulder.

"No – 'cause you de *baby*!" Thornton hisses back, kicking at a clod of dirt as he shuffles listlessly to the row he's working for another bundle of tobacco leaves.

When Fanny arrives with a kettle at the spring-fed well reserved for the plantation's slaves and livestock, Henry is already gulping thirstily from the mossy white oak bucket he's just drawn up with the windlass.

"You gonna puke drinkin' lak that," she says solemnly. Stopping to catch his breath, Henry mimes throwing up into the bucket, but Fanny is too hot and tired to be either amused or disgusted. "I needs some a dat fo de kettle."

When her brother again pretends to vomit into the half-full bucket, Fanny reminds him, "You spose t' be gathrin' kindlin."

"You said I was gonna puke," replies Henry, performing the routine for her once more. But Fanny steadfastly refuses him satisfaction.

Half an hour later, John, a wizened, gray-haired slave

in his late 50s, is washing up after work from a wooden tub in front of his rickety one-room cabin on slave row as he watches Jane limp down from the big house. Alcohol, hard work and the sun have aged John beyond his years, most of them spent here on the Harness plantation in Bull Creek, Virginia. Harness gave Jane to him sixteen years ago after selling Justin, the father of her four eldest children, down the river.

Though Jane and Justin had jumped the broomstick, Harness's disregard for the traditional African wedding ceremony is typical of slaveholders when auction time comes around. Many won't even permit the formality of marriage among their slaves, and those who do would never allow it to interfere with their own claims. But Jane has never loved another man after her husband was taken from his family. Besides, she's always been far too independent to live with a messy, unkempt man like John even though the kind old slave is the father of her three youngest children. Jane and her family have continued to occupy their own cabin, and John visits only for sex, which isn't very often these days.

Over the years John has become Solomon Harness's occasional drinking buddy, of peach brandy and whiskey converted from the greater part of the corn crop that is neither eaten, ground into meal on the plantation's horse-turned grist mill nor fed to the livestock. Although most of the distilled spirits are shipped in barrels to thirsty towns along the Ohio, the two men share a nip now and then. Harness's religious wife Emily won't allow him to drink in their home, and the formality if not the social distinction between slave and master has gradually broken down over brandy and corn liquor during long hours on the riverbank or in John's funky, littered cabin when the weather is bad. He's half lit now, as usual.

"Howdy, Gal, what be on yo min'? Got you some time

fo me?" he asks Jane, his foolish grin revealing a mouthful of bad teeth beneath benevolent old eyes.

"Go shush now, you funnin' me," she replies, knowing John has occasionally been seeing Lizzie, a much younger mulatto woman, for the kind of time he has in mind.

"We could sho 'nuff *have* us some fun."

"Massa Harness want you up at de big house," says Jane, refusing to be drawn into his banter. She's not sure even John knows about tonight though it was he, bless his good heart, who opened her eyes and set things in motion. She allows herself, or is unable to prevent, a mental image of their procreation – for such their sex has always been for Jane: woman's sacred work of begetting. And though this is what Harness wants as well of course, in compelling her to lie with John, providing her master with offspring of their union is as far removed from Jane's willing participation in the act as is loyalty to Harness from her nature. In procreation Jane is moved by some message or promise from her soul or ancestors, the living presence beyond this unending round of toil and exhaustion to which she turns in mute appeal again and again. The source of energy behind her responsiveness to John has always been *opposition* to slavery and Harness's hold on her.

Opposition which if not entirely conscious is nonetheless both total and implacable. Obedience isn't loyalty – and sex, childbirth, mothering are all part of the core of her life that Harness can't touch, can't even perceive. They are Jane's lifeblood, her sustaining spring from a deep-flowing underground river. What Harness and his like see are only where the waters spill out and moisten the earth. Plantation life is the slowly spreading stain the waters make on the land – the rich soil, the hard packed earth, the rock – while beneath the surface flows the river, most of the time beyond Jane's thirsty reach. But her children are wells sunk beneath the bedrock. And it's through each of them that her lifeblood comes back to her, through every one of them that her desiccated spirit survives.

Chuckling softly, John pats Jane on her ample rear-end and reaches for his coat. She gives him a weary smile, of tolerant resignation rather than real affection, before walking in her slow deliberate way to the plain, clean dirt-floored cabin she shares with her children on slave row. Jane has been a slave now on the Harness plantation for thirty-one of her fifty years, having been purchased at the age of 19 with her mother, brother and ten other slaves at an auction in Richmond, Virginia, in 1812 – two years after Harness bought the land the plantation now occupies. She has walked with a slight limp ever since being kicked by a horse during an attempted rape some 20 years ago. If it's likely that only her children would call Jane pretty, perhaps that's because it is they alone who see the real, whole woman. Anyone can see how she has assumed her departed mother Hannah's stout figure, but for Jane's children Hannah lives still in their mother's rare and precious smile.

Only the harvest sees Jane in the fields anymore. Relying on a keen instinct for avoiding trouble, she has risen to the level of a benevolent tyrant among her fellow slaves since becoming mammy to the Harnesses' three youngest children several years earlier. She presides over slave weddings; enforces attendance at church service except at harvest time and in inclement weather; and metes out justice when rules are broken. For all her good intentions, Jane is perhaps rigid to a fault, for once a Harness slave gets on her bad side she can be unforgiving.

Jane draws her authority from her duties in the big house and being privy to whatever news and gossip she manages to overhear. Don't let her thick slave's dialect fool you; to survive and protect her children, Jane finds solutions to critical problems, faces down her fellow slaves and masters, on a daily basis. If she is superstitious, she is also intuitive, street-smart where there are not yet many streets, and river-wise. She often boards steamboats on the Ohio to sell eggs and fresh meats from the plantation, and not all the money gets back to Emily Harness. But Jane knows how much she can afford to put away for her family's needs, and how often she can do it, without being caught. She gleans frontier tales from the slaves and pioneers and river-boatmen on the Ohio as well. And she can read some, having long made it a point to eavesdrop on the Harness children's lessons whenever possible and cleverly manipulating them to pass their book-learning on to her – as she in turn has secretly passed it along to her own children.

Having never experienced freedom nor much solace from her prayers, Jane has stoically endured slavery as her place in life – while not for a minute accepting it – until just recently. Solomon Harness, her current master, is a successful planter who maintains a severely patriarchal, frequently tyrannical relationship with his 61 slaves, many of them born here. But if you do the work demanded of you, life on his plantation is tolerable enough most of the time, unless you happen to cross Jeb Porter. Slaves in border states like Virginia know they have it easy compared to those on plantations in the deep South, whose crops – cotton, rice, indigo and sugar cane – are extremely labor-intensive, and whose planters don't hesitate to resort to extreme forms of punishment to get the maximum labor from their work force. To be sold down the river at the slave auctions in Wheeling and nearby Vaucluse, or right off the plantation as is sometimes the case with Harness's slaves, is not just to be torn from the arms of your family but to be consigned to a living death.

Jane's brother Tom swam the Ohio after beating the white overseer he caught trying to rape her. To strike a white man, of course, regardless of the provocation, is one of the worst offenses a slave can commit, and Tom fled for his life. He promised to send back word of his safe arrival in Canada, when he would help the rest of his family escape, but as with Justin, no one's ever heard from him since. Though Jane often thinks of her lost husband and brother and tries to keep their memories alive for her children, it's her mother for whom she still grieves.

Hannah died with the fever winter before last, and Jane still misses the short smiling woman with skin as dark and blue as indigo, a bright cloth tied round her head. Hannah sang every morning on the way to the fields – the rich, melodious words of "Go Down, Moses" warm and soothing as liniment when that lay-about fog still hugged the ground, the chill of its cold hand wrapped around stiff joints and aching bones. Stooped over the needful plants she was cultivating, worming, suckering or picking – in plangent tones which made a church of a tobacco field and, for a while at least, believers of its toiling, nearly naked parishioners – Hannah summoned God's Sweet Chariot to swing low just to carry her people home. And on hazy summer evenings like this when work and chores were done, as the sun lay down its fiery burden beyond the heavily wooded hills across the Ohio, Hannah's deep contralto stirred hearts and lifted spirits: "Follow the drinking gourd," she sang, "follow the drinking gourd, for the old man is awaiting for to carry you to freedom...if you follow the drinking gourd."

2

Slaves on the Harness plantation were seldom chained at night as they were on the Henderson plantation a few miles downriver; and, unlike this particular Sunday at the peak of harvest, Harness's slaves usually received a day of rest on the Sabbath. They had Emily Harness to thank for that. Aside from selling a strong young buck to slave traders from time to time, Harness felt that he treated his slaves decently enough – not that he got much credit for it. In his opinion, the darkies didn't know how well off they were until he had to sell one of them when cash was short. In 1843 with the price of potatoes roughly six cents a pound and a good horse worth about $20, a western Virginia planter might clear no more than $500 a year from the sale of corn, tobacco and wheat. So although he didn't think much of those engaged exclusively in slave-breeding, there were times when Harness simply couldn't afford to pass up the $1,000 or more a prime male slave would bring. If scenes of families being torn apart – men, women and children being dragged aboard steamboats in chains to be shipped downriver – were sometimes almost more than he could stomach, what of that? A man couldn't afford to let himself get soft. Sentimental. It was a business decision pure and simple.

His plantation had at one time been part of George Washington's extensive holdings along the Ohio, purchased around 1770 when the 38-year-old Virginia legislator journeyed as far west as what is now Gallipolis, Ohio, in search of new land. Washington had surveyed much of the same territory some twenty years earlier for the first Ohio Company. In 1810 Harness, the land's third owner, bought a thousand fertile acres of bottomland and wooded hills at the mouth of Bull Creek in western Virginia's Wood County, seven miles north of the little settlement of Williamstown. Across the river to the south, at the confluence of the Ohio and Muskingum Rivers, was the bustling river port of Marietta in the free state of Ohio.

The proximity of free territory was, in fact, on Harness's mind this hot, humid Sunday evening. The Underground Railroad, active by now in both North and South, was well established on the other side of the river. Washington County and much of southeastern Ohio were being settled by self-reliant European immigrants and New Englanders to whom the institution of slavery was an evil belying their new nation's promise as a land of freedom. More than once Harness had been compelled to gather men and take the ferry at Marietta into relatively hostile territory seeking fugitive slaves belonging to him, and he hadn't always come back with them. He didn't relish the thought of having to go through it all again, not so much because of the trouble involved as the risk of losing his property – to say nothing of the substantial reward he'd have to post.

A lean imposing man in his late 50s, about six feet tall with a hard, humorless face, Harness was sitting at the dusty, cluttered roll-top desk in his library, tallying figures in his ledger. Lying next to the smudged, stained pages of his accounts was an advertising circular for next week's Vaucluse slave auction.

"Come in!" he snapped in response to the tentative knock on the closed door.

Jeb Porter entered, holding his hat. "You wanted me, Mr. Harness?"

"Joo-ly wa'n't the month it should have been, Mr. Porter," Harness replied at once, without greeting or preamble. "You ain't gettin' enough outa yer niggers."

Porter was never summoned to the big house for praise or social conversation; he was expecting a reprimand of some kind. "It ain't from not tryin', Mr. Harness," he said defensively. "I got some a the laziest niggers on God's green earth out there."

"If slaves liked to work, I wouldn't need an overseer, Mr. Porter," Harness said, cutting him short. "But that's not why I called you in here. Close the door."

It would have been hard to miss the relief which flickered across his overseer's face even if Harness weren't the careful observer of human nature that had made him a successful businessman. There were Virginia planters who knew more about soil or weather or growing seasons than he did, but few who got more return on their investment. After Porter took a seat in the straight-back cane and cherry wood chair indicated, Harness continued in a lowered tone of voice: "If I can get a decent price for 'em, I intend to sell Jane's two oldest at the slave auction next week."

Having just been chastised for his lack of production, Porter was unable to contain himself. "But them's two a the best I got!"

Harness overlooked the transgression. "I expect they'll bring close to a thousand dollars apiece," he agreed in a tone of irony.

"But you just, you just done told me we're not gettin' enough work done as it is," Porter sputtered.

"Which is exactly why we need the money these two will bring, Mr. Porter, replied Harness coldly. "I don't cotton to slave breeding, as you know – and I don't like losin' good field hands. But when my overseer can't get me decent profits outa my tobacco, then I have to cover expenses where I can."

"Yes sir," said Porter sullenly.

"Now...I don't know how they find out, but they most generally do. You'll need to watch Alfred and Augustus real close the next few days."

"It's spyin' abolitionist scum tips 'em off," muttered Porter.

"Whoever it is, you'd best sleep light till the auction. I'll be lookin' t' you if any of my slaves swim the river."

"I'll see to it, Mr. Harness." As Porter left, he nearly bumped into John, hovering hat in hand in the hallway just outside the library door. John spoke up immediately, ignoring the overseer, when Porter snarled at him.

"Massa, Jane say you want ol' John."

"Come in, come in – close the door behind you," replied Harness impatiently. The two men eyed each other warily despite the easy familiarity between them. "...You been my faithful slave for a long time now, John," said Harness, his tone of command leavened with genuine fondness for the old man. "I want you to be my eyes and ears for awhile. Let me know if you see any a the niggers actin' restless or suspicious, you understand?"

"Yassuh, massa," John replied, worrying the battered, filthy straw hat in his hands. "These tired ol' eyes an' ears be at yo service." Grinning and ducking his head, deferential though uncowed, he shuffled from the room to leave Harness with his book work.

Meanwhile, in a thatch-roofed lean-to otherwise exposed to the elements, where the cooking was done on slave row, Jane was tending a kettle in which a stew of potatoes, garden vegetables and pork, if you could find it, simmered over an open fire. The heavily perspiring woman beside her was baking cornpone in a crude oven made from slabs of sandstone held upright on the ground by heavier stones at their base.

"Sho is humid," she said to Jane. "Fog gwine be right

thick tonight."

But Jane was too distracted to reply. She jumped when Henry dropped an armload of kindling next to the kettle.

"...That'll do!" she snapped at him. "Go pick greens with Fanny." She returned his questioning look with a scowl and emphatic gesture toward the large kitchen garden the slaves all shared.

The choice for Henry was an easy one: linger here against his mother's wishes to satisfy curiosity and concern over her uncharacteristic behavior, or take flight and lose himself in the rows of poke and collard greens, sweet corn, radishes and melons, under the eyes of no one but his sister. Watching her youngest boy give way to headlong abandon, Jane sighed, unconsciously lifting her eyes to the slave cemetery in a chestnut grove beyond the garden – to one rough wooden cross too small and distant to see from here. Her lined face relaxed, her tired dark eyes softened and liquefied as trees and markers gave up her mother's indelible image.

In some long-ago season of ripe tobacco, Hannah was working the same field Jane's family had labored in since sunup on this long grueling August day. Standing erect to stretch the muscles of her back and shoulders, Hannah gazed out over the blue river, shimmering northern boundary of the plantation, Virginia and the South. Suddenly, as though aware of her daughter's presence across the years, Hannah turned and looked in Jane's direction, gesturing in the slow motion of dream toward the Ohio.

"*Now*, girl!" said a voice, *Hannah's* voice, distinctly in Jane's mind. "Don' you be afraid."

Gasping, Jane tottered, thrusting an arm out for balance, her other hand over her heart.

"Is you all right?" the woman beside her asked in alarm.

"...Sho, I's all right. Jest a little dizzy," Jane heard herself reply, drawing with a deep breath from the same deep well of resolve and replenishment that had sustained her and her children for so long. Then returning, shakily, to the kettle to serve the slaves arriving to be fed. By the time her children came through the line she had regained a measure of composure.

"Ah'm got de hunger, Mama!" declared Alfred with a broad smile, his day's work finally done.

"You always hungry, boy," Jane replied wearily, though grateful for this familiar conversation in the real world, "but you never git no meat on dem bones."

"Never you min' 'bout dat, ol' woman – jes' throw some a dat stew an' pone on mah plate."

As Alfred walked with his modest helping to the shade of the towering sycamore where the family customarily shared their evening meal, Thornton danced up bowing away exuberantly on his battered old fiddle, a present from Emily Harness for Jane's two musically inclined sons. Augustus, Thornton's teacher, was the other.

"Sit'n yo slim butt down and eat!" commanded Alfred. "Don't feel like list'nin' to no jig tonight!"

Thornton reluctantly laid his precious instrument beneath the tree to get in line behind his two elder sisters, who were more withdrawn and secretive than usual this evening. Observing Rachel's attempts to improve her sister's sullen mood, Jane said nothing when Caroline refused to meet her eyes. She noticed after filling her daughters' plates that Rachel was having no success until Caroline finally spotted the handsome young man she'd been longing to set eyes on all day. When she and James exchanged a fond look, Augustus guffawed and slapped his friend roughly on his muscular bare shoulder.

"Car'line got you makin' eyes lak a fool, Jame. She have you jumpin' the broom wif her any day now."

"You just sorry cause she's yo sister," said James, shaking him off.

"Not cause I can't jump no broom wif her. Dat gwine be *yo* mis'ry."

The thought of being married to Caroline made James's smile even broader and less discreet. But it didn't keep him from trading good-natured punches with Augustus.

"*Mis'ry?* You don't know what you sayin', 'Gustus."

"You the one don't know – don't know mah sister laks I do." The look he gave his friend was one of genuine pity. But James's expression said just as clearly: "And you don't know her the way *I* do."

The two of them got their food and joined Caroline, Rachel and the others in the shade. The affection among her family made Jane's eyes shine for a moment as she ladled out stew for the rest of the slaves. Then her deep thoughts recaptured her attention, and her dark seamed face remembered the mask her hard life had made of it.

3

John was relieved to see three slaves approaching the plantation still (to which he had one of only three keys) stealthily through the trees. "Evenin', gen'mun," he greeted them. "Y'all come fo some a Massa's 'liquid courage'?"

"Ef that be corn liquor, that's what we here for," one of them replied.

John poured each a half pint or so from a jar that looked as if it hadn't seen soap and water since the still was built. "*Courage* what you need whar you goin', Hershel. An' a whole lot of it."

"Well then, guess I'll takes a little right chere."

"Save that fo tonight," John advised him. "Git on now 'fo Jeb Porter come nosin' roun'. Massa done tol' him keep his eyes op'n till de auction."

"How you know dat?" asked Caleb.

Chuckling, John said, "Drink too much moonshine, you go blind. Guess Massa think he drink enough wid ol' John by now, I leastways be *color* blind."

The others joined in John's amusement. "Seems t' me, *Massa* be da one mos' affected. His tongue must get t' waggin'."

Alarmed by Caesar's boldness, John replied, "You nevah heard dat from ol' John."

"No, an' I ain't gone blind yet neither," said Caesar. "Massa don't share his moonshine wif me. But I knows you done he'p a lotta folks run."

- 17 -

"You best he'p yourse'f tonight, Caesar. An' dat fambly – dat's who I skeered for. Watch over dem chirren, you hear?" With surprising strength as well as concern in his eyes, John directed this command to all three of the men.

"Course we will," promised Caesar.

Downstream from Bull Creek the steamboat Lady Byron, captained by Joseph Sterrett of Louisville, was tied up at the bank as transparent wisps of mist begin to veil the river. Sterrett knew that in the Ohio Valley this time of year fog could become opaque and oppressive enough to enshroud his deck, let alone the deceptively slow-looking current. Two old slaves sat on a clay bank above the wagon track down to Bull Creek, watching the spectral vapor rise over the river. They'd been on the plantation for more than half a century, since 1793 when President Washington himself still owned the land and they crossed the Appalachians among a group of slaves and overseers sent to clear bottomland along the Ohio for farming.

Marietta, the oldest organized settlement in the Northwest Territory, had already been established five years before their arrival by 48 pioneers led by Rufus Putnam, one of the founders of the second Ohio Company. The party of boat builders, blacksmiths, carpenters and surveyors had floated down the Ohio River in flatboats from Pittsburgh. But the pair of slaves had witnessed nearly everything else of historical significance in the Ohio Valley since the coming of white and black men to the American frontier: the end of the bloody Indian uprisings which terrorized the first settlers, in 1794; Ohio's statehood in 1803; and the beginning of steamboat traffic on the Ohio River around 1810, the year Harness took possession of the land that had become his 1,000-acre plantation – a mile from where the great Shawnee warrior Tecumseh had killed his first white man at the age of 16.

Perhaps the most meaningful event in the lives of the two slaves, however, had been the development of the Underground Railroad, which began after the American Revolution and moved west with the settlement of the Northwest Territory. It was with the help of the Underground Railroad that Jane's brother Tom had fled to Canada after swimming the Ohio River 20 years ago. Though the time had long since passed for these two to attempt such a daring undertaking, they'd heard talk the past couple of days, which they fervently hoped would come to nothing, of another planned escape. It was one thing for a strong man on his own to take his life in his hands; for a mother, even a woman as strong and courageous as Jane, and her seven children to take such risk was just plain crazy. Better that Alfred and Augustus, whose impending sale was rumored, accept their fate rather than endangering the lives of their whole family.

The two elderly slaves had been alerted to the possibility of an escape attempt with the visit last week of Rial Creadle, southern Ohio lawyer, country doctor, schoolteacher and textbook distributor. Unbeknownst to his planter customers throughout western Virginia and Kentucky, Creadle was an ardent abolitionist who found the idea and practice of slavery so morally repugnant he risked his life every time he ferried across the Ohio to sell books – for he came not only as a representative of eastern publishers but as an undercover agent of the Underground Railroad.

In addition to a pleasant and profitable visit one rainy day with the Harnesses and their five children, Creadle had been able to give instructions to Alfred while having his horse shod, a fortuitous opportunity afforded by the rain, Creadle's ingenuity and Alfred's position as Solomon Harness's blacksmith. Earlier in the week – the same day he had warned their mother of Augustus and Alfred's pending sale at the slave auction – John had put word out on the Underground Railroad as well, passing the information along to a fellow slave entrusted with the plantation's weekly shopping in Marietta. There the news had been relayed to David Putnam, Jr., the community's most outspoken abolitionist and unofficial leader of the local branch of the freedom line. Putnam, Creadle and others had quickly decided that a book-selling expedition to the Harness plantation was in order; Creadle would try to find some way to encourage and assist in the young men's escape.

With, typically, no specific stratagem in mind – for improvisation was both virtue and necessity in the unstructured operation of the Underground Railroad – Creadle had awaken on the morning of his ostensible sales call to a moderate but steady rain which looked as though it might last all day. If so, Harness's slaves would most likely be put to work in a multitude of accumulated agricultural and domestic tasks under roof rather than in the fields, which they would otherwise quickly turn to mud. And Alfred would be at the forge.

When Creadle rode in on his big sorrel gelding, leading a pack horse loaded with textbooks and other wares, the rain had become a light drizzle which could not deter Emily Harness and her four younger children from greeting him with their usual excitement.

"Fanny, bring an umbrella so Mr. Creadle's books don't get wet," Mrs. Harness ordered Jane's youngest daughter, who was enjoying her rare day off from field work in the big house. The slave who had announced their visitor held his horses, and under Emily's protection, since Fanny was too short to provide the umbrella's shelter herself, Creadle dug out books he thought the children would like. He chatted with their fine-featured if somewhat frail-looking mother after asking to speak to Harness about his horse.

"The children so love it when you pay us a visit, Mr. Creadle," Emily told the bookseller, dispatching Fanny to fetch the master. "You've helped make readers out of all of them."

"Much obliged, Mizz Harness. That's what makes all those long hours in the saddle so worthwhile," he replied, always more at ease in her company than with her husband. "The older I get, the more I appreciate Shawnee's single-footin' gait, but I guess too much of a *rocking chair* would rattle a body some."

Emily Harness, obviously cultured and well-educated, in whom one could perceive both pride and (Southern) piety, was gracious enough that at one time Creadle had asked himself whether, if it were up to her, there would be any slaves on the Harness plantation. That was a long time ago, not so much in years as in what Rial Creadle had learned about slavery from those fleeing it.

"How do, Mr. Creadle." Solomon Harness and his eldest son came striding around the corner of the two-story brick manor house, made of clay from creek banks right here on the plantation. The walnut structural timbers, oak floors and paneled interior walls were rough-hewn products of the plantation's sawmill, on Bull Creek. The severely handsome building bore the Greek Revival style: post-and-lintel doorway flanked by sidelights beneath a long rectangular transom, with windows topped by a single limestone lintel. It had replaced the original log cabin Harness built before bringing Emily to the site and had been enlarged twice, with a second wing making an "L" of the original "I" shape, followed by the addition of sleeping porches for the region's many hot summer nights.

William, 17, having shown little interest in his studies at the university in Charlottesville, was being trained to assume as many of the management duties of the plantation as his capabilities would allow.

"I hear you may have need of my blacksmith," said Harness by way of greeting.

"I do, sir," replied Creadle. "My single-footer's off on his gait. His left front shoe's come loose."

"My house slave will see to it, Mr. Creadle."

"Thank you kindly, Mr. Harness, but I'd prefer to take Shawnee down to your blacksmith myself. I know he's competent; I'm just kind of particular that way."

"Of course," said the slaveholder. "A man can't *be* too careful about his horse, now can he? You know the way. Go tell Alfred to attend to it," he told the slave, "then see that Mr. Creadle's pack horse gets watered after Mizz Harness has the books she wants."

Creadle thanked Harness again, told Emily he'd be back to do business when his horse had been shod, then led the gelding down a gentle slope past the plantation's summer kitchen, spring house, privy, and granary to a large Applachian-style horse barn that was more than twice the size of the house. The blacksmith shop occupied one end of the barn. At the opposite end, above a double-door through which Creadle and the horse traded the overcast afternoon's gray mist for the dark pungent interior of sweet-smelling stalls and tackroom, the peaked roof was extended to support a block and tackle with which hay was lifted into the loft. The feed boxes had recently been filled, and a number of healthy well-tended riding, carriage and draft horses were too busy eating to take much notice of the visitors.

Creadle knew Alfred by name and description but not by sight. Nor did he have any way of knowing for sure whether Jane's oldest son was aware of the book peddler's role with the Underground Railroad, let alone his real reason for being here. Did the unfortunate slave even know he was about to be sold down the river?

Alfred knelt to inspect the shoe pointed out to him,

which Creadle had pried loose himself before riding onto the plantation. The young man's hands were light but sure in their touch, and the horse soon relaxed as the blacksmith went from hoof to hoof with his quick expert examination.

"You'd be one of Jane's sons if I'm not mistaken," Creadle said in a tone of voice which anticipated and tried to minimize the slave's response: one of instantaneous suspicion if not alarm.

"Yassuh, massa," said Alfred guardedly, keeping his eyes on his work as he pulled the loose shoe, cleaned the gelding's foot, then rasped away some excess hoof. Creadle observed intently as the young man measured the shoe against the hoof, then brought it to a bright red glow in his forge before beating it with a few precise blows to match the reshaped hoof. Was Alfred's obvious strength more than just physical? Could he stand up to the demands and danger of escape?

Creadle was pleased though not particularly surprised when the blacksmith proceeded to pull the right-front shoe as well and repeat the whole process with deft quick movements which soon had Shawnee leaning against his handler in sleepy contentment.

"You've got a real knack for this work, Alfred," Creadle continued, unable to detect a reaction to his use of the slave's name.

"Yassuh, massa," said Alfred.

"Josephus *told* me you were a damn good blacksmith. It's a comfort knowing Shawnee's in such capable hands."

This time Alfred tensed and paused for a moment, still not looking up. When he resumed, the cadence of his work had slowed; Creadle could sense the wary listening of his whole body. And the moment was no less dangerous for Creadle himself. If he were unmasked somehow through the slave's fear or awkward responses later to any questions put to him by Harness, or by outright betrayal, Creadle wouldn't be the first agent exposed in this way. A beating and indefinite sentence in a Virginia prison would be the least he could expect. On this side of the Ohio his life was at risk, as Levi Nutter's family in neighboring Ritchie County could attest. Four of the Nutter sons were murdered for helping runaway slaves escape. So was Ritchie County abolitionist John Wass, while Doddridge County innkeeper Luke Jaco lost a leg after being shot and left for dead because of his Underground Railroad activities.

But this was also the best opportunity Creadle could have hoped for to pass along the information he'd come to deliver. Alfred's response to the name Josephus, known to slaves and abolitionists alike as "the Ferryman," for rowing more slaves to freedom than any ten men along the Ohio though he was a slave himself, was enough to push Creadle across an invisible line both men could now sense.

"I'm with the Underground Railroad, Alfred," he said, speaking rapidly but deliberately. "I've come to tell you that we have reason to believe you and Augustus are going to be sold at next week's slave auction. But there are good people both black and white across the river who want to give you a chance to escape, if you're willing to risk it."

Alfred was frozen, kneeling in the dust beneath the horse.

"Keep working, someone may see us. I'll tell you what you need to know while you finish shoeing Shawnee. You've got to act like that's all you're doing – we're just passing the time of day, understand? Keep working." Though Creadle said this in an urgent undertone, his gestures and posture projected a practiced nonchalance that no more told the truth of his emotional state right now than it did of Alfred's. Who now hesitantly, awkwardly resumed the task at hand. By rote he pulled the remaining shoes, cleaned and rasped the hooves, then reset and clinched new nails in the shoes he'd removed. While Creadle told him where and on what day and at what time Josephus would meet the brothers and ferry them across the Ohio to freedom – not *down* the river to the deep South, where they'd be ground to pieces in the maw of plantation agriculture.

"But I don't wanna run, Mama! Dey catch us fo sho, den Massa gwine sell us down de rivah."

"You hush now, Car'line! We ain't gwine get caught."

There was little privacy under the best of circumstances on slave row. Jane had just stunned her family, gathered in their one-room cabin after dark, with the announcement of their attempt to escape this very night. Alfred and Augustus were the only ones who'd known, and they and their mother were having difficulty now in getting the rest of the family to keep their excited voices lowered.

"Caught or eat up by snakes or wil' animals," insisted Caroline.

"Dat's just what Massa say, Car'line, t' keep slaves from runnin'."

"Dere's wolves an' bears and painters in dem woods, Alfred, an' you knows it!"

"Ain't no animals gwine jump a wagon full a people," he insisted.

"Bounty hunters sho 'nuff will."

"Aw, you ain't skeered too is you, Thornton?" Augustus chided his younger brother.

"I ain't afraid. Jus' sayin' what could happen."

"I ain't gwine lie to y'all," Jane interjected. "It's true we takin' a risk. But we be on de Underground Railroad all de way to Canada."

"A *real* railroad, Mama?" asked Henry.

Alfred and Augustus both laughed at Henry's innocent misconception, but Jane treated the question seriously.

"De Underground Railroad's *people*, Henry. Black an'

white folks dat knows slavery's wrong. Dey'll hide us durin' de day an' take us from place t' place at night."

Jane had been aware since well before this evening's supper of a conspiracy of silence between her eldest daughters. Now, with this revelation of her own, the air of secrecy between them had become as thick and heavy as the humid, fetid air in the sweltering cabin.

"...You best tell her, Car'line," Rachel suddenly blurted out during a lull in the family's heated whispering.

"Best tell me what?" asked Jane, already anticipating the answer.

"I hangin' a baby, Mama!" announced Caroline in an anguished tone of voice.

Jane felt her insides go queasy. It was not that the news surprised her; Caroline had been spending much of what free time she had, after her field work and chores were finished, with James. The strapping young man reminded Jane of Justin sometimes. But the timing of her daughter's pregnancy could hardly have been worse. Tonight they were going to cross the Ohio to freedom. Not *try* to cross, Jane couldn't allow herself to think in terms of might or maybe; these were the lives of her whole family she was risking. Though Master Harness was a more lenient man than Jane's previous master, there was nothing that upset him more than a runaway slave. Once when a boy named Sam ran off and got caught Harness had branded his forehead with the letter "R", then sold him down the river. Jane could still smell the seared flesh. And this was not one slave she would be depriving Harness of but eight! Caroline's pregnancy probably wasn't far enough along to pose a real problem, but it was another life in Jane's hands.

And it wasn't just her enraged master that concerned her, or the bounty hunters who would come after them drawn by his big reward. In 1843 the virgin forests of the Northwest Territory were indeed still full of wolves, bears, bobcats and "painters" or panthers. Though Alfred was correct in pointing out that these predators seldom attacked humans unless provoked or in defense of their young, like most slaves Jane had been sheltered from the wilderness all her life. And like the typical planter Harness found it advantageous to stoke his slaves' superstitions and fears of wild animals to make escape attempts appear as dangerous as possible. He was a good storyteller, especially when his tongue was well lubricated with corn liquor. And his tall tales of runaway slaves being torn to pieces by wolves and bears when they had foolishly ventured into the wilderness beyond the Ohio were even more effective when delivered by Harness's drinking buddy, John.

But the alternative to the family's escape was the certain loss of Alfred and Augustus to plantations in the deep South. From what Harness had unwisely let slip a few days ago while drinking with John, there would be nearly fifty slaves for sale, some chained together in droves from as far away as Clarksburg, at the slave auction next week at Vaucluse. Ever since John had shared with her the grim news that the Master intended to sell her eldest when the tobacco was cut and hung, Jane had been laying a few things aside to take with them. Then yesterday afternoon she'd baked twice as much cornbread as usual, half for their trip. When the girls had noticed and asked questions, Jane put them off in her stern maternal way. They were apparently too caught up in their own secret to have become suspicious about hers.

"...I knowed you an' Jame was up to somethin'," she reassured Caroline now. "How far along is you?"

"'Bout three months, I reckon. Me an' Jame was gwine jump the broom. Now, jus' lak me, mah baby's never gwine know its daddy."

"No! *Not* like you, Car'line," Jane contradicted her. "Yo baby's gwine grow up *free*, girl. If'n yo Jame be the man you think he is, he'll fin' a way too. We get word to him somehow."

But Caroline was not placated. "He ain't gwine *fin'* me if we all split up down south – where we all be dead soon anyway," she lamented. "Why can't we stay where we is, Mama? I hear dis ain't nothin' lak dem cotton and cane plantations."

"Cause dat's jus' where yo brothers headed."

"*Massa gwine sell 'em at de auction*?" exclaimed Rachel.

"Dat's what John say," affirmed her mother.

The family shared a moment of stunned silence before Alfred spoke up: "Only we ain't gwine *be* here. Rial Creadle done tol' me ever'thin's all set – when he here the other day to see Massa."

"*Rial Creadle*? You mean de man dat sells Massa books?" asked Thornton in surprise. "He wif de Underground Railroad?"

"He sho 'nuff is," replied Alfred. "He say a boat be ready t' take us across de rivah *tonight*."

For the first time Fanny spoke up: "What we gwine *eat*, Mama? Where we gwine sleep?"

Jane lifted the corner of her straw-filled pallet to reveal the hidden cache of cornbread.

"This be fo tonight. We be fed an' sheltered 'long de way."

For a moment no one had any more to say. Jane surveyed the dark interior of the cabin, feeling rather than actually seeing the expressions on each of her children's faces. "We through talkin," she said. "Gots t' git ready now."

"...Can I go say goodbye to Jame, Mama?" asked Caroline finally in a tone of sorrowful resignation.

"Go wif her, Gustus," said Jane. "See he don' make a fuss."

4

The fog continued to roll in, and by ten o'clock visibility along the Ohio had diminished to just a few feet. At the Box Plantation a few miles downstream, a wiry old slave pushed off from the bank in a large rowboat and began to row hard against the current close to the bank.

Upriver, Jeb Porter lit an oil lamp and stepped outside to make his nightly rounds of slave row.

At about the same time, Augustus, with Caroline huddled beside him, knocked softly on the door of James's family's cabin.

"...What is it, 'Gustus?" asked James, sensing at once upon opening the door that something was wrong.

"Tell him, Car'line."

"...We runnin', Jame!" cried Caroline.

"*Runnin*'? '*Cross de river*?" His hoarse whisper of disbelief stabbed Caroline like a boning knife. She could only nod, while Augustus mastered the impulse to hang his head in shame by holding a desperate and steady gaze on his best friend's bewildered eyes.

"But...why you nevah tol' me?"

"I didn't know, Jame! Mama just done tol' us."

James looked to Augustus for an explanation.

"Massa fixin' t' sell Alfred an' me at de next slave auction. He done tol' me I dassn't even tells you, Jame."

"*Come wid us, Jame!*"

Augustus grabbed her arm to object, but it was

unnecessary. "You knows I can't leave my ol' mama, Car'line," James wailed softly, his voice restricted to one high keening note in his swollen throat. "She be dead within de week if'n I go."

"Oh, baby," sobbed Caroline, "I carryin' yo chile!"

"You *what*?"

Suddenly the sound of footsteps. A bobbing yellow light burned dully through the fog. James opened the door wide and all three crowded through it with noiseless urgency.

"Who is it, Jame?" A woman's tremulous voice from a pallet on the floor.

"Shhh, Mama!"

The three of them huddled together just inside the door of the dark, musty cabin lit by a single wavering candle. They hardly dared breathe as Porter's footsteps stopped in front of the door...then trailed off, muffled then consumed by the fog.

"...You...?" Unable to speak, James made a swollen belly with his arms.

"You nevah tol' him?" asked Augustus incredulously.

"I...was...goin' to," Caroline managed to choke through her sobs. Embracing her, James too was now crying. Distressed to the point of tears himself, Augustus put an arm on a shoulder of each of them.

"She tellin' de truth, Jame. Dis all happen de las' day or two, and we dassn't tells a soul. I knows you can't go wid us so I nevah said nothin'. But I swears as yo frien' we get word back t' you when we safe in Canada."

Augustus gripped James's hand and arm, then turned his sister around to face him. "Car'line, we gots t' go," he told her firmly. But James tightened his arms around her. Caroline looked desperately from one man to the other, from her lover, her lost husband, to her brother.

"Dis crazy, 'Gustus! Y'all be caught fo sho. Den

whupped an' sent down de rivah. What gwine happen to Car'line an' my baby den?"

"No one gwine stop us, Jame, not even you. Now turn loose of her....Turn loose of her, Jame."

James glared defiantly at him for a moment, then released his grip and looked longingly into the eyes of the woman about to leave him.

"I see you again, Car'line. You tell me where you is, and I be there soon's I can....Dis safe, whar you goin' wif my woman, 'Gustus? You promise you gwine take good care of her?"

"I'll take care of her, Jame. Underground Railroad take good care of all of us."

Caroline reached out to James, and the only life she had known, one last time. Then she and Augustus slipped noiselessly through the door and were swallowed up in the night.

Cursing the fog that had slowed his rounds, Jeb Porter suddenly spotted movement in front of him. "Who's that? Hold it right there!" he commanded.

When he got closer he recognized John. "What're you doin' out after dark?"

"Jes' lookin' out up at de still. Massa ax me t' keep an eye on things."

"That don't give you no call t' be out after dark. I could put some stripes on yer black ass fer that."

"Yassuh, I specks you could."

"Don't think just cuz you an' Mr. Harness is 'drinkin' buddies' that you're anything but a nigger t' me, boy!"

"No suh, I don't think dat fo a minute."

"Don't think you're somewhere I cain't git to you."

"I don't think dat neider."

"And don't git smart with me, boy!"

"Oh, I de dumbest niggah on dis here plantation,

Missuh Porter. I don' get smart wid nobody."

Porter glared at him, suspecting he was being mocked but not certain enough of it to risk incurring Harness's anger from what he might consider an unnecessary beating. "You *think* yer a helluva lot smarter than you are, old man. Someone around here's got big eyes and a damn big mouth, and you know what the hell I'm talkin' about."

"Yassuh, Missuh Porter – I don't know *what* you talkin' 'bout."

"Talkin' about what's gonna happen t' you if any a Mr. Harness's niggers tries t' cross the river. If my whip don't git you, some accident will. You understand me?"

"Yassuh, I understands dat all right."

Porter pushed him aside with contempt and walked away. John, making no effort to regain a dignity he had never lost in the confrontation, looked after his antagonist with serene indifference.

Around midnight, Jane and her family wrapped the few things they were taking with them in rags and crept from their cabin into the stifling, humid night air. Holding hands to stay together, they slipped quietly toward the river.

At the water's edge, Hershel, Caleb and Caesar were just now pulling Josephus's rowboat up onto the muddy riverbank.

"No sign a Jane an' her chirren," Caesar announced.

"Dey don' come soon, I takes you three an' comes back fo de res'. Can't take ever'body at once nohow."

"How you git us to de udder side in dis fog, Josephus?" asked Hershel nervously. "Cain' hardly see nuffin'."

"Don' hafta see it. I knows where it is don't I?"

"But how you know which way we headed?" asked Caleb.

"Current tell me. Y'all afraid, I kin take dat fambly fust."

"No, no! We ready!" the three of them replied almost in unison.

Suddenly Jane and her children appeared atop the slippery riverbank, and the two younger boys came sliding down to the water's edge. Alfred helped his mother make a cautious descent over entangled roots and debris, and the rest followed. Jane was unpleasantly surprised to see the other three slaves. In fact she was having second thoughts about going through with their plan, because the river was literally invisible to them in the fog. They could smell its pungent, fishy odor and hear it lapping against the bank, slapping the sides of the boat, but they could barely make out one another or the bobbing rowboat itself. How could they possibly make it to the other side, more than a quarter of a mile away? How would they know they were even heading in the right direction?

"John nevah tol' me y'all be goin' wid us," she said.

The three slaves shared a look among themselves, and Hershel replied, "Y'all be goin' wid *us*."

"How we all gwine fit?"

"Makin' two trips t'night," said Josephus. "Pray de Lawd no one be missin' you fo a while."

The words had no sooner left his mouth than the sound of men shouting and the baying of bloodhounds reached them faintly through the fog. Porter had found their cabin empty and raised the alarm – there was no turning back now.

"Git in, git in! Dey comin'!" Jane ordered her family.

"Hold on! You cain't all go!" protested Josephus.

But the panicky slaves ignored him and clambered aboard, dangerously rocking the boat. Many of their bundles were dropped on the riverbank or in the swirling muddy water. Wading into the river, Caesar helped Jane and the younger children aboard until everyone but him had squeezed into the nearly swamped skiff. With no room for him, he pushed the wallowing boat away from shore.

"Go on, Josephus, row! I hold on best I can."

"Damn fools! We all gwine drown!" raged Josephus.

"No we ain't – we gwine make it to de udder side!" vowed Jane. Now row, niggah! You chirren bail wid yo hands! Like dis! *Bail*!"

The boat was already taking on water. Behind them they could hear the muffled, urgent voices of Harness and Jeb Porter, under the keening of the plantation's hounds. Josephus pulled on the oars with all the strength in his work-hardened body; they felt themselves leaving the near riverbank, and the plantation where most of them had lived their entire lives, behind. They could sense the overloaded rowboat gradually entering the strong steady current of the main channel.

And now the fog which had appeared, and in fact remained, a threat to them was their protector as well. Harness, Porter and the dogs had reached the water but they couldn't see the fugitives gliding silently toward the middle of the Ohio.

"*Come back here, you fool niggers, before you all drown*!" shouted Harness.

Though somewhat muffled by the fog, the Master's furious disembodied voice sounded closer than it was because of his invisibility. A moment later the sudden loud report from his flintlock rifle nearly swamped them as the slaves all ducked reflexively.

"Ohh, *now* we in trouble!" moaned Caroline.

"Don't you worry none, Missy," Hershel tried to reassure her. "Massa wouldn't aim t' hit us if'n he could see us. We too valu'ble. Ain' dat right, Caesar?...Caesar?"

"He ain' chere!" cried Caleb.

"...Maybe he gwine *swim* to de udder side," offered Henry hopefully.

"...Caesar cain't swim a lick," replied Hershel.

The prolonged silence which followed was broken only by the scraping of oars against oarlocks and Josephus's grunts and labored breathing as he struggled to pull the foundering boat through the water.

Then, remembering the mortal danger they were in, Jane commanded again: "*Bail*, y'all!" while scooping cold water back into the river with her cupped hands.

"Don' be rockin' de boat!" hissed Josephus.

"Bail an' don' rock de boat!" Jane hissed back. Following her example, the others resumed bailing with hats or hands as Josephus strained mightily at the oars.

Although rowing blind, he found the river to be a reliable guide. The moment he pointed the skiff's nose up- or downstream, the current magnified the deviation and tried to swing the boat around: clockwise or counter-clockwise, respectively. His passengers all continued to bail as best they could.

"I think it's workin'!" cried Augustus. "Don' you Alfred?"

"Sho it's workin'!"

"Well don' stop!" urged Jane. "Keep chuckin' dat water!"

For nearly half an hour no one spoke another word or so much as whimpered. At last, however, Fanny could contain herself no longer. "How wide *is* dis rivah?"

"Seem like we been on it fo hours," added Henry.

"Whole lot better'n bein' *under* it, ain't it?" grumbled the oarsman.

"What you think, Josephus?" asked Alfred.

He didn't answer at first and Alfred assumed he'd been ignored. But then: "Current say we nearly dere. Hear dat soun'?"

Again there was silence in the boat as its occupants strained to hear what Josephus was talking about. And soon they could all hear it: the welcome sound was unmistakably the lapping of water against the bank, against land, *free* land, on the Ohio side of the river.

5

"Praise de Lawd!"

Neither completely afloat nor quite submerged, the swamped little vessel under the precarious command of Josephus the Ferryman nosed into the mud and sand of the Ohio shoreline. Sand and gravel grated against the bottom of the boat, amplifying the sense of arrival; the fugitives could literally feel free land in their bones. After what had seemed like hours on and in the water, they were at last at rest, unmoving. For a moment they were all too stunned – in Josephus's case too exhausted – to move or say a word. Then the jolt of landing on an impossibly distant shore elicited Jane's benediction.

Alfred slid over the side of the boat to steady it, and Hershel and Augustus were right behind him. Together they pulled it up onto the bank and the rest followed. Jane, the last out, helped by her two eldest sons, immediately dropped to her knees and prostrated herself on the packed wet sand, her broad shoulders heaving soundlessly. When she looked up to her children standing over her in anxious attendance it was through eyes overflowing with a reverent gratitude they had never seen before, though they would come to realize that they had each imagined or intuited it. For the expression had always been latent in the weary resignation in their mother's features, a prefiguration of the fulfillment of Hannah's dream – a shadow or reflection of the inconstant but abiding faith that had sustained Jane all these years. "Praise de Lawd!" she said again, in a voice all the more fervent for the self-restraint imposed upon it.

"Dis here's free land, chirren!" she proclaimed in a loud whisper. "Le's say a prayer now fo Caesar. He done give his life he'pin' us git across."

After Josephus and his passengers had bowed their heads, Jane struggled to her feet and extended her arms to the oarsman.

"Bless you, Josephus! You done save my fambly."

"I only done what I knows is right, Mizz Jane."

Alfred and Augustus each gripped a hand warmly; Josephus humbly accepted their mute show of gratitude.

"Why don' you excape yose'f, Josephus?" asked Thornton.

"Oh, de Box Plantation ain' a bad place fo a nigger t' live," he replied. "'Sides, if'n I run, who be left t' row folks like you 'cross de rivah?"

Augustus put his big hand on Thornton's head. "Guess you nevah thought a dat, huh?"

"Y'all he'p me push dis boat out. I's got t' git back fo I's missed," said Josephus.

Men, women and children all had a hand in pushing their rescuer's now relatively light and bobbing boat back into the Ohio's strong current.

"Is we safe now, Mama?" asked Henry in an incautious tone of voice which presumed the affirmative. Called "Jane's Shadow" by some of his siblings and others on the plantation because he was seldom far from her side, Henry was always asking questions, prompted by his curious nature and a vivid imagination. Until old enough for field work he was always with his mother at the big house, where like her he'd learned to read and write from the Harness children.

"Shush, boy, you want de bounty hunters t' ketch us? We be in danger till we in Canada."

There was no sign of the lantern that David Putnam, Jr., their conductor, was supposed to be swinging to mark the beginning of their journey on the Underground Railroad. They didn't dare call out, for fear not only of bounty hunters but any venal citizen interested in what was bound to be a big reward for eleven escaped slaves.

"...What we do now?" Jane whispered to Hershel and Caleb.

"Le's split up," suggested Hershel. "Me an' Caleb'll go downstream, y'all head north. Whoevah runs into Massa Putnam kin fetch de res'."

"Dat soun' good t' me, Mama," Alfred agreed.

"Alright den. We follow you and 'Gustus. Watch where you walkin'," she told the younger children. When Jane and her family had vanished in the fog, Hershel and Caleb reached almost reflexively for the flask each had managed to hang onto during the scramble for the boat and the perilous crossing.

"Fo Caesar," said Hershel. The fear in the men's faces turned to sadness when they made eye contact. Then, retreating to the privacy of their own thoughts, they pocketed their flasks to head stealthily downriver.

Vegetation was thick on both sides of the Ohio; the going would have been difficult in broad daylight. After they had struggled for half an hour or more along the riverbank with no sign of a lantern or their conductor, the combination of fog and corn liquor began to disorient the two fugitives. They decided to strike out on their own for the Little Muskingum, a much smaller tributary than its namesake farther downstream. Having accompanied Harness and Jeb Porter to this side of the Ohio for supplies on occasion, they were somewhat familiar with the lay of the land, and they had been told that the Little Muskingum pointed the way to the Jewett Palmer Station on the easternmost of the three main lines of the Underground Railroad in Washington County.

*   *   *

In the meantime, a short distance upriver from where the two parties had separated, Henry was the first to spot a lantern glowing dimly in the fog.

"Dere's de light! I see de light, Mama!" he whispered in excitement.

In response to Alfred's passable imitation of a hoot owl, the light swung back and forth.

"Dat be him!" confirmed Augustus with an intense feeling of relief.

"Glory, glory!" Feeling faint, Jane gathered her strength, and her family was soon face to face with David Putnam, Jr., a tall lean man in his mid-30s. His eyes widened when he saw the number, and youth, of the fugitives, but he held his tongue.

"Dere be two more downstream a ways," Jane told him breathlessly.

"Well, we can't look for them now," said the abolitionist. "If we don't run into them on the way to the wagon, I'll send someone to look for them. Now take hands, and...beee...qui-et."

In single file, Putnam led the family on a dizzying trip through the fog. A quarter of a mile upriver they encountered, first in ghostly outline, a canvas-covered wagon hitched to a matched pair of draft horses standing impassively in the traces, their only movement the rhythmic flicking of their tails to ward off the night's mosquitoes.

"Women inside," said Putnam. "You'll make your first stop just before daylight. The Palmers will feed you and hide you till dark. We're going to do everything we can to give you a safe trip to Canada."

Jane and her three daughters clambered in beneath the heavy tarpaulin, stiff with the fog's residue. Henry and Thornton were unaware of their mother's and sisters' discomfort, sandwiched between the oppressive weight of the damp canvas and the hard, springless wagon bed. To the tired boys the wagon represented a cozy place to sleep while the men of the family would have to walk all night. They exchanged a rueful look as the driver, a taciturn man named Stephen Quixote, gave the reins a shake. Then, with the four brothers following on foot, the fugitives set off for the Jewett Palmer farm on the first of what would be many harrowing wagon rides if the family were to reach Canada safely.

A Freedom Journal
Caroline Pope, 1853

Much as I come to hate lying all covered up in the back of a wagon, and neither flood nor fires ever going to make me do it again, its the seat upside the driver or I'll walk thank you, the night we made it cross the river then saw that lantern light waving out there in the dark all by its lonesome, thats the first time I think maybe Mama know what shes doing after all. When we climb in that wagon the underground railroad done send for my family thats when I first believe maybe theres really people this side of the river cares if we live or die.

I tell myself right then only I still don't really believe it that somehow my baby and me going to make it to Canada. I didn't even want to go, not if my man couldn't go with us. I tried to get Mama to forget this crazy idea but Alfred and Augustus would be sold down the river, thats what they said and Mama feared its so. They wouldn't none of them hear of us staying, I was the only one crying out against crossing that great dark river which very nearly did kill ever last one of us.

But when we get safe across, all except Caesar who did drown, and that wagon come for us like Mama said it would, then I begin to see Mama's side just a little bit. You know she drop right down there in the mud and kiss the ground we standing on when we get shut of that little boat half full of water that Josephus done rowed us across in.

Then the wagon. We cover up with this big piece of canvas with the menfolk walking longside and I sure don't want to be there, I want to be back with my man James, my baby's daddy, but Mama say You hush up Caroline and Rachel too. Fanny she never say much of anything. That wagon starts moving, taking me away from James I know forever but we're safe and alive in the dark under that canvas just like Mama said we'd be and I feel her start to cry next to me. She don't make a sound but her sides shaking and I know what shes doing. Then I see how all along she just afraid as I am and I feel real proud of Mama and feel like protecting her the way she done protect her family all these years. I puts my arm around her and she snuggles up against me like all of a sudden I'm the mama, the way I be my own baby's mama by the time we gets to Canada.

And so I promises myself and the Lord too if Hes listening that if we gets there safe I'm going to write down the story of how we done it, how Mama done save her family even them that ain't born yet from slavery.

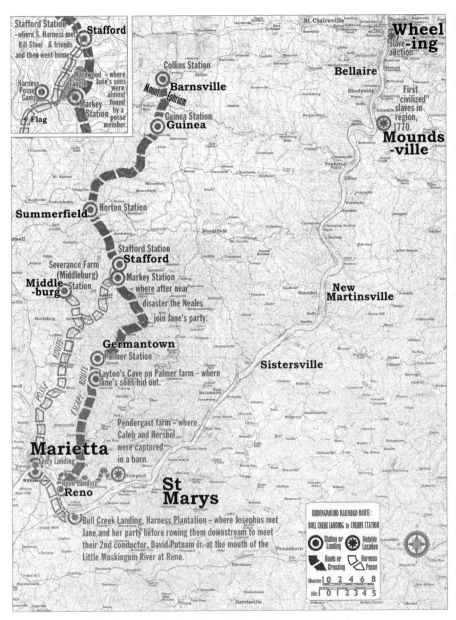

The first six nights of Jane's family's escape: Sunday-
Friday, August 1843

6

Little more than an hour after the fugitives' escape, Harness, Porter and two loyal slaves, surrounded by the plantation's eager bloodhounds, rode up to the ferry in Williamstown, Virginia, with enough commotion to rouse the ferryman from his cabin.

"Guess I don't have t' ask what brings you, Mr. Harness."

"Just git us the other side a this damn river and make it fast!" was Harness's salutation.

When they'd all crowded aboard, the ferryman used a boat hook to raise the heavy underwater rope with which the ferry was pulled back and forth across the river by sheer muscle power and began the long tug to the Ohio shoreline. The horses were always skittish on the ferry, never more so than on pursuits with the near frenzied pack of dogs. The men cursed and fought with the animals while Jeb Porter, a man now seriously concerned about his job security, had also to contend with his employer's cold fury.

"Who the *hell* has a boat around here big enough for 11 slaves, Mr. Porter? *Twelve* countin' the rower hisself."

"May have been more than one boat, Mr. Harness – but I sure as hell don't know whose."

"If'n either a you boys knows anything, you'd best come clean *now*, you hear? This is your last chance," Harness growled at the slaves, who were trying to control the leashed bloodhounds. But as known collaborators with the plantation owner, they were never trusted with information of any kind by the other slaves, and both

Harness and Porter were aware of this.

After disembarking in Marietta, the pursuers' progress up the Ohio side of the river north of town was fairly slow in the heavy fog. They'd ridden a good two miles with no sign of the fugitives when Harness's overseer said, "I thought sure we'd a crossed their trail by now."

"You better hope we cross it soon, Mr. Porter."

"Current not carry dem dis far, Massa," one of the slaves remarked.

"Damn abolitionists might," said the overseer.

"If they were here, Mr. Porter – whether the river or the abolitionists, or God himself brought them here – the dogs would have told us."

Porter said nothing and the two slaves shared a big grin behind his bowed back.

This was virgin wilderness through which Jane and her family were traveling, on a rutted trail little more than a cow path, overhung with vegetation so dense the ground would have been nearly this dark beneath it in the middle of the day. Limbs of the immense trees towering over them had become interlocked over many centuries and in many places were woven together by wild grapevine as ancient as the trees. So dense was the forest canopy that many of these giant hardwoods wouldn't fall even when their trunks had been chopped through unless boys with hatchets had been sent aloft first to sever the thick serpentine vines wrapped around their upper branches.

Intensifying the forest's claustrophobic embrace was the territorial insistence of its invisible legions of insects and tree frogs, claiming not only the teeming, forbidding woods but the oppressive night as well. Their incessant percussive chorus, rising and falling in pitch, unvarying in cadence, was like the porous wall of an endless tunnel through the dark, a sort of skin that seemed to the wary fugitives almost tactile and within reach yet endlessly falling away as they moved through it. As with city slickers, however, what scared these lifelong plantation dwellers most was what they *couldn't* hear but only imagine. Henry and Thornton were clearly fearful, and Alfred and Augustus, each carrying a heavy stick, were hyper-alert. In addition to the infrequent snarl of a four-legged predator – and even more frightening, the scream of its prey – armed bounty hunters might burst from the dark glowering forest at any time. Perhaps it was just as well that the fog still surrounded Jane's family in its clammy blindfold.

Inside the rattling wagon the women were finding no comfort in their bone-jarring ride beneath the stiff wet canvas either.

"Yo on mah leg, Rachel!" complained Caroline.

"Well den move!"

"I cain't breathe in here, Mama!" wailed Fanny.

Jane rose to an elbow, lifting the canvas with her other arm to address her daughters: "Dis de las' time ah'm tellin' you, girls! Yo big gapes git us caught, den what? We got a long trip ahead, an' we gwine be quiet de whole time, you hear?"

She returned to her back with a groan; as the canvas settled slowly down upon her she frowned and sighed deeply. The force of memory rose in Jane like a flood and with both reluctance and relief she gave herself over to it.

...That beautiful, terrible spring day more than 16 years ago. It had been such a long cruel, utterly dismal winter. The Ohio had frozen over twice, turning the river into a jagged plain of ice, a sterile, brittle landscape, dazzling at times beneath a brilliant but frigid sun, which nonetheless reflected the misery of living on slave row in day after day of sub-zero weather.

Yet spring that year had begun with an unusually long

warm spell which thawed the earth and coaxed life back into it earlier than Jane could remember ever witnessing before. Redbud and reckless splashes of wild dogwood were riotous in the woods, while apple, cherry and peach trees spread bright pink and white patchwork quilts over the deep green of the plantation orchard. Overnight life had become full of a promise Jane could almost believe in. Wasn't just being alive in such a spring after the winter her family had endured enough to be thankful for?

That Sunday in late April, with the hills turning a pale green almost before her eyes under the warm touch of the once again life-affirming sun; the scent of wild lilac planted by Hannah years before borne in on a warm breeze through chinks in the log walls of the cabin, the same gaping cracks that had caused such suffering in winter...on that sun-drenched April morning as Jane awoke with a sense of renewal and possibility to songbirds celebrating their annual rite of spring in the white oak branches budding out over the cabins of slave row, Jane's reverie, her tender words and embrace with Justin, her very will to live were all cut short when the door of their cabin suddenly burst open and she realized in an instant of revelation and betrayal that they had come to take away her man.

It had done no good to try to stop them. Harness's men had come prepared for Justin; for all her despair, all her fury, they had flung Jane to the ground like a sack of potatoes: a self-image of futility she had carried with her for years.

Soon afterwards, in Harness's library where she had no business being, Jane had pleaded mightily with the slave-holder himself. "*Please*, Massa, I *beggin'* you! Don' take mah man from me an' our chirren!"

"Now, Jane, you've been a loyal slave – don't destroy your position here over this," admonished Harness, distressed by her presence in his sanctum and by the emotional outburst, but implacable.

Sobbing, falling to her knees, Jane had clutched at his hands. "Massa! I do *anythin*'! I thinkin' of mah chirren, Massa. Dey make you better slaves if'n dey has a daddy!"

"The decision's already been made," he replied, his scant store of patience exhausted. "Now, if you'll –" but his next words or Jane's memory of them had been eclipsed by her uncontrollable wailing.

At the plantation's steamboat landing that afternoon her three eldest children had stood beside her as she held 1-year-old Augustus, to watch Justin, manacled and in chains, being led up the gangplank of a sternwheeler headed downriver. He was shirtless and his broad back bore open wounds from the whip of the overseer who had preceded Jeb Porter. Jane was crying quietly, standing strong for her children's sake. But there was desolation in her heart, and in her eyes the emptiness that still resided there now. Her children's incomprehension, Alfred's youthful stoicism, Rachel's inconsolable grief...Jane remembered all of it – more clearly at this moment than she had in a long time.

Perhaps worst of all had been Harness's "consolation." Noticing Jane and her children clustered atop the riverbank, he'd broken away from his conversation with a swaggering, gaudily-dressed man and come up to comfort her. "Slave dealers," he muttered with an expression of disgust – "scum of the earth....I'm truly sorry it had to be this way, Jane, but he brought the flogging on himself. And you and your children will be well taken care of. I've told John to watch out for all of you. John will give you more pickaninnies than Justin did."

About a mile from its mouth at the Ohio, the Little Muskingum makes an acute bend, doubling back upon itself for a quarter of a mile, then straightening for a half-mile run to the village of Cornerville. Anyone hacking his way through dense underbrush along the winding stream itself, rather than following the wagon track Jane and her family were on, would be hopelessly behind schedule by now, as indeed Caleb and Hershel were. But their situation was even worse than that, for they were unaware that the road to Jewett Palmer's prosperous 150-acre farm left the Little Muskingum at Cornerville to run roughly due north to the community of Germantown in Liberty Township. By now it was growing lighter, the fog had begun to lift, and the two slaves were a long way from the Jewett Palmer Station.

While fugitive slaves were forced to take refuge near the Ohio River on rare occasions, most often they headed for more remote stations like Palmer's, a night's journey north of the border between slave and free states. Although its name conjures a network of tunnels, "Underground Railroad" refers of course to a covert *operation*, with political, religious and moral objectives, rather than to the actual routes fugitives followed. "Stations," the homes of abolitionists acting as station managers, were the Underground Railroad's communications centers. Slaves were seldom hidden there; the stations were too well known and closely watched by those whom abolitionists contemptuously called "lick-spittle," hoping to collect a reward for reporting or capturing runaway slaves. Fugitives were concealed in the hidden chambers of safe houses, in caves, thickets and haylofts.

The principal Ohio terminus, upon which a number of major and branch lines converged northward from the Ohio River, was Oberlin, about 20 miles southwest of Cleveland and half that distance from Lake Erie. The ultimate destination might be Canada; a northern city or some local, usually black community in rural Ohio where the escapees would try to cover their tracks and begin to put down roots; or, with forged freedom papers, the black African colony of

Liberia. Established on the west coast of Africa in 1822 by the American Colonization Society, Liberia was either a new homeland for freed slaves or the final destination in a devious scheme to send black Africans back where they came from, depending on which historical account you believe.

Exhausted, probably hung over and scared, Caleb and Hershel were lost alongside a meandering shallow creek in the dense hardwood forest of Washington County. Caleb took one last swig and tossed his empty flask away.

"Cain' see nuffin in dis damn fog!" he complained, slurring his words.

"No wavin' lantern-light, da's fo sho."

As they picked their way through the nearly impenetrable marshy underbrush, Caleb muttered, "I wisht Caesar was here. He know what t' do."

"On'y one thing *to* do an' dat's fin' someplace t' hide 'fo daylight," replied Hershel.

"Massa Harness have his houn's out by now, I reckon."

"I spects he be at de ferry by now."

"Maybe we lucky," said Caleb. "Maybe de ferry not be runnin'."

"Huh!" snorted Hershel, "Massa Harness be 'cross dat rivah if'n he an' his houn's have to swim. Count on dat."

Unable to continue following the creek, they began to claw their way up the steep, rocky side of the ravine.

"Keep yo eye open fo snakes in dese rocks," Hershel warned his companion.

"I been lookin' out fo snakes since we got off'n de boat."

Climbing out of the timber-choked gully, the runaways suddenly realized they were facing cleared land, and there, looming out of the fog not far ahead of them, was the shape of a large building of some kind. But if they had visions of reaching safety at last, the fugitives had only a moment to savor them. The faint bellowing of Harness' hounds on their fresh trail sent them running for what proved to be a barn. Without hesitating, they dashed inside, scrambled up the ladder to the hayloft, and buried themselves in sweet-smelling clover.

For several minutes that must have seemed much longer to them, all they could do was lie there listening to the dogs getting closer. Their barking had alerted the Pendergast family, lingering over breakfast while waiting for the fog to lift. The 16-year-old eldest son grabbed his shotgun and followed his father through the back door.

Outside, two slaves were attempting to leash half a dozen bloodhounds, all leaping frantically against the closed double doors of the barn, when the dogs suddenly forced open the doors and surged inside. The Pendergasts ducked through a side door to confront Solomon Harness standing at the foot of the ladder to the hayloft, shotgun cocked and ready, staring up into the dark loft. He kicked savagely as the baying, barking dogs milled around his legs.

Above him, Jeb Porter shouldered his own gun and peered into deep shadow. Dawn light filtered through cracks in the walls to reveal freshly-mown hay tied in bundles piled loosely on the floor of the loft...but no fugitive slaves.

"Come outa there, niggers, 'fore I blow your heads off!"

"Don' shoot!" shouted Caleb, emerging from beneath the loose hay like some water mammal surfacing. Hershel surrendered as well and was soon following Caleb down the ladder, with Porter standing over them in the loft and Harness awaiting them on the ground.

"Looks like them two's the only ones up here, Mr. Harness!"

"You make damn sure a that! *Where's the rest of 'em?*" Harness yelled at the slaves. "I want an answer and I want it now!"

"Hold on here!" Pendergast interrupted. "You can't just come onto a man's property and start threatenin' people at gunpoint! I don't care what color their skin is."

"The hell I can't!" bellowed Harness. "These is *my* niggers!"

"You heard my father!" Pendergast's son had his own shotgun leveled at the slaveholder's chest. "You're trespassing on private property!"

Unruffled, Harness replied, "Point that somewhere else if you don't intend to use it."

"Do as he says, boy!"

Young Pendergast looked up to see Harness's overseer standing at the top of the ladder; the boy was looking right into the barrel of Porter's 10-gauge. Hershel and Caleb meanwhile stood frozen on the ladder midway between the loft and the ground.

Startled, Noah Pendergast was nonetheless cool beyond, or because of, his years. "I'll take the head off your friend here first, Sir!" he warned Porter, turning again to the slave-owner.

Before Noah's father could intervene, Harness defused the potentially explosive situation. "Don't fire, for God's sake, Porter! You got grit, son," he praised the boy. To Mr. Pendergast he said, "I'll send my overseer for the sheriff, Sir. No need for someone gettin' shot over a couple a niggers. *Come on down here, you two!*"

They descended shakily. "You not gwine let 'im take us away is you, Massa?" Hershel pleaded with Pendergast.

"I'm afraid that's up to the law," replied the farmer, feeling sick from the arrested violence and its outcome. He was neither an abolitionist nor a sympathizer of slavery. Had he found the runaways in time, he might have been able to help them; as it was, all he could do now was delay the inevitable.

"The Fugitive Slave Law's clear enough about that, I assure you," Harness answered him. "Ride an' git the sheriff, Porter!" Pushing the slaves roughly away from the ladder, he snarled: "One way or t'other, you're gonna tell me where the others are and how the hell you got across the river. You'll save yourselves a lotta mis'ry if you tell me now."

"We don' know *wheah* dey is, Massa! We done got sep'rated," said Caleb, a look of terror in his eyes. Harness knew he couldn't beat any answers out of the slaves here, but he expected to find out soon enough where Jane and her family were headed.

In fact, they had just arrived at the Jewett Palmer farm, its prosperous-looking two-story frame farmhouse, large red barn and cluster of well-maintained outbuildings faintly glowing in the approaching dawn.

"Where the hell you been?" demanded Palmer, a stocky, energetic Unitarian minister in his mid-40s. "It's nearly sunup."

"Couldn't find 'em in the fog," replied Stephen Quixote, the driver. "We was late gittin' started."

"Is this all? I thought there were eleven."

"This was all David had with him."

Alfred repeated for Palmer the story of the missing men while Quixote climbed down and pulled the heavy dew-laden canvas from Jane and her daughters – and Henry, who'd been allowed into the wagon after trudging gamely behind it with his brothers until well past midnight. All four of the children were sound asleep. Jane was wide awake and exhausted.

"Wake up y'all," she told the sleepers. "We here."

7

At the Palmer Station the wagon's passengers were roused first with protests then with apprehension and fear when shaken from their cocoons of sleep and canvas. In the misty gloom before dawn even the moist air full of the freshness of morning was a harsh reminder of the dangerous new life on which they were embarked.

"Land sakes, you folks look exhausted – and hungry too, if I'm not mistaken." Rachel Palmer was an intense but appealing middle-aged woman with a reassuring smile and a large wicker basket of food, covered with an immaculate white cotton napkin. "C'mon with me," she told Jane and her family; "we have a place all set up in the barn for your breakfast."

The pungent interior of the big red two-story barn was fragrant with hay, feed, leather and the various hardwoods of which it was constructed. The exposed posts and beams were walnut timbers; the stalls, feed boxes and troughs were all oak; while the rough plank sides had been cut from tulip poplar. Awaiting them in one of the stalls was a bright wool blanket spread out on a layer of fresh straw. Mrs. Palmer handed Jane the basket with a smile such as the lifelong slave had never received from a white woman before. Had she not been so concerned with the welfare of her children, and tired and hungry herself, she might have been disconcerted by this profoundly alien expression. Could it and its wearer possibly be trusted?

"Nothin' fancy, but it'll help fill you up, said Mrs. Palmer, interrupting Jane's thoughts."

"Thankee kindly, Mizz," Jane replied.

"When you're through eating, Mr. Palmer will be out t' hide you and your children 'round the farm. You'll have all day long to sleep – looks like you could use it."

"Yes'm. Mah boys sho can – dey done walk all night."

"'Cept fo Henry," teased Thornton – "he slep' wif de girls."

"Did not! Just restin'," said Henry, still too sleepy to muster much indignation.

"How many more nights we gwine hafta walk like dat, Mama?"

"Lots mo, Thornton, best git used to it," Alfred chided him.

"Don' rightly know, son," replied Jane, looking to Mrs. Palmer for an answer.

"It'll probably be close to three weeks before you get to Canada," she said sympathetically.

"*Three weeks*?" exclaimed Thornton. Although no one else said anything, it was obvious that the whole family was disheartened by the information. But hunger prevented them from dwelling on it for long. While Jane and her children were wolfing down their breakfast of ham and eggs with slabs of bread and fresh fruit from the Palmers' orchard, the wagon was concealed in an outbuilding. Then Palmer and Stephen Quixote led the draft horses to a nearby watering trough.

Jewett Palmer, of medium height and build, was a man large in principles, with the courage and will to uphold them. Born in New Hampshire in 1797, he was an intelligent, serious reader, educated on his father's farm. At the age of 16, he'd joined the New Hampshire Volunteers and fought in the War of 1812, returning to the family farm after his discharge. Five years later the Palmers began a move to the American frontier, arriving in southeastern Ohio in the spring of 1818. His family had no doubt instilled anti-slavery sentiments in Jewett at an early age, as the Palmers were closely related to William Lloyd Garrison, leader of the abolitionist movement and a founder of the American Anti-Slavery Society. In their new home they were soon exposed to the northern exodus of fugitive slaves crossing the Ohio River from western Virginia into Washington County on the way to Canada.

Twenty years ago Palmer had married Rachel Campbell and the couple settled on a farm that became their first Underground Railroad station. Palmer soon gained respect as a community leader; industrious and upright with an unwavering sense of moral judgment, he always had a helping hand for the downtrodden. By 1830 he was operating the second Palmer station, a few miles north of the first, where Jane's family had just arrived.

"Damn shame about the one man drowning," he said now to Stephen Quixote, the wagon driver. "That's the first passenger we've lost in a long time. God rest his soul, he'll be better off than the other two if Harness finds 'em before we do. What do you suppose happened to them?"

"I figure they just got lost. Fog was thicker'n granny's Sunday gravy last night, even if they'd known where the hell they was goin' – which of course they didn't."

"Well, if Harness got 'em, we'll know soon enough," replied Palmer.

Even sooner than he imagined, for at nine o'clock the same morning, in a spacious high-ceilinged room of the Washington County Courthouse in Marietta, a special magistrate's hearing had just been called into session under Judge Ben Cotton. Word of the slaves' escape was already in the streets and shops, homes and taverns of the town, and the visitors' gallery was full of the local citizenry most vocal on the issue of slavery vs. abolition.

"Do you wish to represent yourself in this matter, Mr.

Harness?" asked the black-robed jurist, an imposing man with a thick mane of nearly white hair and intelligent if rather unfeeling blue eyes.

"I do, your Honor."

"And you're here in behalf of the Washington County Anti-Slavery Society, Mr. Putnam?"

"Yes, your Honor," replied David Putnam, Jr., notified just an hour before of the runaways' capture on the Pendergast farm north of Marietta.

"Will you please tell the Court what happened, Sheriff?"

Washington County Sheriff Jesse Loring was a rangy man who looked a lot bigger than he was while in fact being tougher than he looked: quite an accomplishment since even miscreants ignorant of his reputation usually crossed the street to avoid him.

"Well, your Honor, Mr. Porter here rode in about seven o'clock this morning and said that a couple of Mr. Harness's runaway slaves, here present," – Loring gestured to Hershel and Caleb – "was out at the Pendergast farm. Mr. Harness wanted to take 'em back across the river to Virginia. But Mr. Pendergast objected, claiming Mr. Harness was trespassing on his property, so Harness sent his overseer in to get me. I rode back out with Mr. Porter, and we come straight back here to the courthouse with the accused."

"Is that the way you would describe the incident, Mr. Pendergast?" asked the Judge.

"Purt' near, your Honor. Though I will say that Mr. Harness's overseer drew down on my son with a cocked and loaded 10-gauge."

This was received in the gallery with a murmur of indignation, followed immediately by muttered epithets of support for Harness, but Judge Cotton silenced both sides with his stern cautionary gaze in that direction. "Do you wish to press charges, Sir?"

"No, I reckon not, your Honor."

"Do you have papers, Mr. Harness, documenting your ownership of these slaves?"

"Right here, your Honor," replied the slaveholder, handing them to the bailiff, who glanced at them before passing them on up to the Judge.

"Which one of you is Hershel?" asked Judge Cotton, scanning the documents with a practiced eye.

"Da's me, yo Honah."

"And you're Caleb?"

"Yassuh."

"...Everything seems in order here for Mr. Harness's return of his lawful property, under the Fugitive Slave Law of 1793," said the magistrate after further examination. "Do you wish to address the court in this matter, Mr. Putnam?"

"I certainly do, your Honor," replied Putnam, rising. "As you know, Sir, the United States Supreme Court's decision in Pennsylvania last year made it very clear that states are not obliged to enforce this odious piece of legislation, and a number of northern states no longer do. I propose this particular incident as a test case of whether the free state of Ohio is going to follow the moral lead of its brethren states in the Union, or continue to acquiesce in the abominable practice of slavery."

There was a smattering of applause and, again, comments both pro and con concerning Mr. Putnam's remarks; this time the judge made his point with his gavel.

"That's for the state of Ohio to decide, Mr. Putnam, not this court. I hereby issue a warrant for the arrest of one Hershel and one Caleb – the legal personal property of Solomon Harness of Bull Creek, Virginia – and direct you, Sheriff Loring, to return the aforesaid slaves to their rightful owner forthwith. Next case."

The eruption in the gallery couldn't be dealt with so summarily this time, despite repeated poundings of Judge

Cotton's gavel.

"It's a moral outrage! A sin against God!" shouted a dignified, portly matron one might have thought above such public display.

"You heard the Judge – it's the law, lady. Nigger's no different 'n a man's cattle!" countered a drummer of hardware and farm supplies who was lodging at the Mansion House, a hotel on the Ohio River levee.

"*Well, I...!*"

"*You're a disgrace!*" trumpeted the town's Presbyterian minister, who looked prepared to remove his collar and take on his parishioner's antagonist right here in the courtroom. But, other than in the unfortunate slaves, the decision aroused little emotion amongst those actually involved in the hearing, most of whom appeared to have expected the outcome.

After their big breakfast, Jane's physically and emotionally spent family were dispersed to hideouts around the Palmer property to rest during daylight. Most of Palmer's neighbors knew or at least suspected what went on at the farm, they just didn't know when. Some of them would have gladly turned in the fugitive family for what Harness would later announce as a $450 reward; with labor worth less than a dollar a day, that represented more than a year's income for many local farmers.

Stephen Quixote was asleep in the haymow in the barn. Jane and Caroline had bedded down in a pine grove a short distance from the house. Nearly invisible beneath the overhanging boughs of the trees, Caroline was sound asleep, but Jane stirred restlessly, her fitful slumber disturbed by a cough that had come on during the night. Rachel, Fanny and Henry lay hidden in a thicket near their mother, while the three older boys were hiding out in a cave half a mile from the house. Palmer made it a point to work around the farm in plain view of passersby, partly to paint a business-as-usual picture and partly to keep an eye out for bounty hunters.

About two p.m. an abolitionist named Julius Deming rode in on a well-lathered horse to report what had happened to Caleb and Hershel. He found Palmer and his hired hand inside the barn replacing the wooden slats of a false-bottom wagon that would be used if the fugitives had to be transported in daylight.

"They caught two runaways from the Harness Plantation out in Reno this morning," Deming announced before dismounting.

"What happened?" asked Palmer.

"Judge Cotton turned 'em over to Harness. Talk is, he'll be comin' after the rest with a posse."

"Them slavers don't know when to quit, do they Jul? Give your horse a rest and come up to the house for a cuppa coffee."

Having slept soundly all morning, Rachel and Fanny now lay awake talking. Fanny was nestled against her older sister, her head supported by Rachel's arm.

"What you spose Canada be like, Rachel?"

"Cold for one thing. I hear tell it snow dere all de time in de winter."

"Ohh, dat be *nice*," said Fanny.

"Nice an' cold," replied Rachel with a distinct lack of enthusiasm.

"Mama say we be free in Canada."

"Dat's right."

"...What dat be like – free?"

"Mean we live like white folks. Nobody tells us what t' do."

"...We can do anything we wants?"

"*Any*thing," said Rachel firmly.

"...We can eats meat ever' day, an' weah fine clo's, an' go t' church?"

"Well, no one say we cain't. No one tell us we gots t' work all de time – who we gots t' live with. Cain't sell us t' no one an' take us away from our fam'ly."

Although there was a look of wonder on Fanny's face as she daydreamed next to her sister, on Rachel's there was sorrow provoked by the litany of freedom's gifts she herself had enumerated. In her mind's eye now, as if inspired telepathically by Jane's earlier reminiscence, was a child's exaggerated perspective of an enormous steamboat, smoke curling ominously from its towering stacks, attached to the riverbank by a gangplank on which her bleeding, manacled father was being led away from her forever.

May 8, 1864

My Dear Brother Thornton,

I came out of my bedroll this morning the same way I woke up at the Palmer farm after that first night of our run for freedom. Like falling from some great high place. I was dreaming about being back in Virginia, only I was free to move about and see what interested me. Everything else was just the way it used to be. You and Mama and everyone else in those tobacco fields with old Jeb Porter the devil himself riding over you. But in my dream I could go wherever I wanted to. I knew Jeb nor anyone else could make me do a damn thing I didn't want to so I was traveling all over that plantation, the way you can do in dreams. I was floating down Bull Creek to the river in old man Harness's skiff, knowing he would never catch me at it, then across the fields (no boat just wings I guess) over the heads of you tobacco pickers. But later I saw myself down there cultivating and suckering the plants, pulling the shoots out by the roots the way Jeb Porter was always threatening to do with slaves who wouldn't work hard enough. But I didn't have to work in my dream, so I left Jeb Porter and the little boy that was me behind.

Do you remember how beautiful that infernal cage of ours could be at times, Thornie? The shade trees hanging out over Bull Creek to meet in the middle above that clear shallow water where you and I used to catch lizards and crawdads on Sundays? Remember how cool it could be in the heat of the summer, how some days we would spend every minute in the fields wishing we were standing up to our knees in the creek? Or how we would look south out over those green and yellow fields of tobacco and mustard seed at the ridgeline a half mile or so from the river and talk about how that was all that stood between us and the cotton plantations down south we were always hearing about? I used to think they were right there on the other side of those hills. I could never understand all the talk about being sold down the river when we could end up over there any time, a short wagon ride away, if we weren't careful. My ignorance of geography may be what kept me from getting into any more trouble than I did.

I also dreamed of how it was between you and me, Thorn. How you were my older brother but I was the ornery one and how that sort of evened things out in all the ways we were always trying to be better than the other one. I miss you, brother, like I still miss Mama after all this time. I don't know how closely you've been able to follow the fighting and have no way of knowing if you've received any of the letters I've written (3 I think) since the 27th Regiment, Infantry, of the US Colored Troops was organized in Delaware, Ohio in January. But as I'm sure you know by now, we were ordered to Annapolis long before we were ready in anything other than our eagerness to fight, and we've been on the move in Virginia ever since, which is why I've written so little. But other than the occasional skirmish the closest the 27th has come to the battlefield is guarding troop and supply trains with enough success to offset our heavy losses as we push on to Richmond. At least that's what they tell us, do you read anything different in the papers? Here in the middle of the action – no, not even in the middle but on the very edge of it – it's hard to know what's really happening in the grand scheme of things if in fact there is one. War, I'm learning, is far too complex for the individuals involved in it to truly comprehend.

Since Mr. Lincoln saw the light a second time (the first being his Emancipation Proclamation of course) and replaced that cautious old Mrs. Meade with Gen. Grant as general in chief of all Union armies, it hasn't been difficult to understand Confederate strategy. Aside from keeping themselves between us and Richmond they're trying to hold out till Northern voters have had their fill of dying white sons and elect George McClellan in November to lead this divided nation to compromise and peace – and a return to slavery?! – instead of victory for the Union and the fulfillment of freedom's promise for all Americans. Needless to say, dear Thornley, toward that end we of the 27th, and the USCT in general, are dying to get into battle in equal measure to our courageous fellow soldiers who are dying in it. It's way past time for Johnny Reb and the Jeb Porters and Solomon Harnesses of the world to learn who they've been keeping in chains and randomly, thoughtlessly killing and abusing for so long. Hoping you are in good health and spirits and sending a prayer my way from time to time, I am,

your loving brother,

Henry

8

After each lash of Jeb Porter's long whip Solomon Harness questioned the captured slaves in turn, an interrogation carried out at the top of his lungs.

CRACK! "*Where'd they go?*"

"*Don' know, Massa!*"

CRACK! "*...Which way they headed?*"

"*Please, Massa, don' whup me no mo!*"

CRACK! "*...Who took you 'cross the river?*"

When John entered the decrepit little outbuilding used for imprisonment on the plantation, around which hovered an almost perceptible aura of pain and suffering, mocking sunlight streamed through the open door onto Hershel's and Caleb's flayed backs. Their arms were painfully outstretched, their hands tied to a roof beam of this small shed where beatings were formally administered.

"Posse here, Massa, an' yo ho'se is saddled," he managed to get out, shuddering at the sight of the ravaged flesh.

"That's enough for now!" snarled Harness. To John he said, "If you can't git any answers out of 'em, let 'em hang here till I get back."

"...I have you down soon as dey's gone," he said in a low voice hoarse with emotion after Harness and Porter had left.

Outside, a dozen or so riders sat astride their horses, made skittish by the smell of blood.

"Bring my horse up to the house," Harness told John.

"Ready for some coon huntin', boys?" cried Porter, shaking the dripping blacksnake whip at the posse.

"Yeah!" "You damn right!" "Ready for some a that *re-ward* too!"

Harness was met by Emily on the verandah. "How long will you be away, Mr. Harness?"

"We're takin' provisions for three days, Emily. But with any luck, I'll be back tomorrow."

"I sure hope you find Jane. I don't see how I can manage without her."

"Well, I may let you keep *her*, but her whole damn family's gonna learn the high price of ingratitude."

"Whatever do you mean?"

"Down the river – ever' last one. These stupid, lazy niggers have got to learn not t' run off on me, Emily. I'm tired of chasin' after 'em."

"Fiddlesticks. There haven't been that many runaways. Most of them like it here."

"Most of 'em don't have sense enough to – Jane's kin in particular."

"If you're talking about her brother again, Tom had good reason to flee."

"He didn't have the *right*, Emily!"

"No need to raise your voice, Mr. Harness....I trust you'll leave the drinking and carryin' on in Ohio to your vigilantes."

Offended by his wife's insinuation, Harness didn't deign to reply. John led his big high-strung bay stallion up and held him while the slaveholder swung gracefully into the saddle.

"Good-bye, Emily," said Harness, touching the brim of his hat. "William's in charge while I'm gone," he told John. "See that Mizz Harness is well taken care of."

"Yassuh, Massa, I'll see to it," said John.

Harness pulled the horse around and cantered down to the waiting posse. Emily watched him leave with an all but unreadable expression which appeared to possess respect if not quite affection...then caught John watching her and returned with dignity to her own realm: the big house. At least the responsibility of running the plantation for a day or two would be good for their eldest son.

When John returned to the shed where the slaves were strung up, Hershel was still on his feet, but Caleb's legs had buckled and he was hanging by his manacled hands.

"Cut 'em down!" John ordered one of the slaves who had accompanied Harness and Porter across the river earlier.

"But Massa said –"

"*I* said cut em loose!" John repeated in a voice steeled with rage. When the slave hurriedly complied, first Hershel, then Caleb collapsed into John's arms. He helped the exhausted men to lie face down on the dirt floor, then ripped his rag of a shirt in two to place beneath their heads. "You gwine have to stay locked up here," he told them, "but I'll bring you water and some of Hannah's poultice fo dem cuts."

In the meantime at the Palmer farm, Jewett Palmer accompanied Julius Deming to where his rested horse was tied to a hitching post next to the watering trough.

"Tell David we're sorry to hear about the two that got caught," said Palmer. "The eight here seem to be in good enough shape to move on to the Markey Station after dark."

"You think Harness'll be out lookin' for 'em tonight?" asked Deming.

"My guess is he'll stay in Marietta tonight. Let his posse have some fun first, then get a fresh start in the morning."

"Well, if we can just keep the damn bounty hunters off

their trail..."

"Bounty hunters and some a my neighbors. A few of them aren't above kidnapping *free* Negroes for the kind of reward Harness is likely to offer."

Deming shook his head in disgust. "I'll let David know, Jewett."

Palmer waved and took his hat off to wipe the sweat from his forehead, then dipped his handkerchief in the trough and laid it against the back of his neck. August in the Ohio Valley, where small talk this time of year was sure to include the rhetorical question: which is worse, the heat or the humidity?

Late that afternoon Harness's posse rode into Marietta with a combination of arrogance and country-boy-in-town anticipation of a hot night on the levee – drinking, gambling and carousing in the waterfront area's numerous saloons and brothels. Several riverboats a day docked at the levee, disgorging a constant stream of rough men looking for a good time and the fancy women paid to give it to them. The riders' first stop was the livery stable.

"You boys be spendin' the night with us?" asked the owner.

"Only if my Creole honey locks me out!" crowed James Lee Forrester, a handsome young Virginian who fancied himself the dashing cavalry officer – and who would in fact ride with Morgan's Raiders some 20 years later.

"*Your* honey? Yours and 5,000 other guys'," one of his fellow riders ragged him.

"Not when *I'm* in town!"

"This all be on you, Mr. Harness?" asked the stable owner.

"Long as they don't tear up the place," he said. "I'll be stayin' across the street."

"I hear you're after a woman this time – a woman and her seven kids."

"That's right. We already caught two others. One fool nigger drowned tryin' t' *swim* across."

"He musta wanted his freedom real bad," declared the owner's son, despite a warning glance from his father.

"Well you tell the good people of Marietta that I'm offerin' a $450 dollar *re*ward for the return of the lot of 'em. I figure folks around here could use that kinda money real bad too."

"Four hundred and fifty dollars?" The owner uttered a low whistle, and Harness could see dollar signs flare up in the man's shrewd eyes.

"Why git 'em all riled up, Harness?" asked the posse's eldest rider, a neighbor of the Harnesses who eked out a living for his ragged family by digging "sang" or ginseng, hunting, trapping and the occasional share in a reward offered by one of the area's slaveholders. Common labor, after all, was for slaves and he couldn't afford any. "We'll be bringin' 'em in ourselves this time t'morrah."

"You'd better, if you want a share a that *re*ward, Mr. Seevers. Spread the word, will you?" Harness asked the owner. "I don't care who finds 'em – long as you bring 'em back alive."

As soon as their horses had been tended to, the men hurried out onto Ohio Street to start spending the money Harness had advanced them. One group led by Jeb Porter headed for the nearest saloon, while another was soon ogling the gaudily illustrated poster in front of Big May's. **"COME MEET OUR BEAUTIFUL CREOLES! ALL THE WAY FROM NEW ORLEANS!"** it proclaimed, but few of the men were paying much attention to the words.

Big May was an ample light-complexioned woman of German or Scandinavian heritage who looked and sounded just like her name. Hers was "the bordello among Ohio

Street's brothels" according to the business cards she distributed to her clientele. Several prostitutes with shades of skin color ranging from white through high yellow to cocoa lounged about in two large parlors of rococo splendor, laughing and entertaining customers.

"*Where's my Orleanna*?" boomed young Forrester the moment he walked through the front door.

Big May's look of annoyance turned to amusement when she saw who her loud visitor was. "She's with a customer, Darlin'," she welcomed him in a voice even louder, deeper and more reverberant than her client's. "But she'll be down in a few minutes. She's missed you."

"What'd I tell ya?" Forrester gloated to his companions. "I can wait," he announced to the madam. "She'll be with me the rest of the night."

When she laughed – a hearty resonant laugh from deep down in that enormous bosom of hers – Big May's eyes almost disappeared in the folds of her fat rouged cheeks. "If you got the money, honey!"

...On the verandah of the Levee House Hotel just down the street, Solomon Harness sat down with a cigar to watch the street scene and sip from his flask.

In the background, river traffic varying in size from canoes to stately sternwheelers and dowdy freight-hauling side-wheelers cruised past on the Ohio, blue and placid on this bright sunny afternoon. Wafting off the five-mile bend in the river on whose northern bank Marietta was situated was a deliciously cool breeze, for which the white and free black stevedores and heavily guarded slaves loading or unloading steamboats moored at the levee were even more grateful than Harness was. Wagons, carriages, riders and pedestrians – few of them women and those mostly at work, attempting to separate the river-faring men around them from their money – passed in front of him on the wooden sidewalks and in the dusty street. Smoke from cooking fires even on this hot August day drifted upriver, teasing the nose with the aromas of meats, casseroles and freshly baked bread.

With a mixture of distaste and annoyance, Harness watched an old black man named Jeb Coursey shoveling horse-droppings from the street into a wagon pulled by a team of mules. "That's all free niggers is good for," he groused to himself. Then noticing yet another copy of the *Marietta Intelligencer* being waved excitedly in front of the rare person who hadn't already heard about the daring escape of Jane and her family, he tossed his cigar stub angrily into the street and stomped into the hotel for dinner.

Back at the Palmer farm, Jane's three eldest sons were sprawled on deerskins in a shallow cave hollowed out over time by the erosion of what was now a meandering little stream called Whipple Run. Although Alfred found their hideout damp and gloomy, to his younger brothers it was a cool sanctuary from the August sun.

"You rather be out in de fields, slappin' black flies?" asked Augustus in a tone of disbelief. With a flat creek stone for a pillow, he reclined in obvious comfort, insulated from the cave's cold rough floor by the supple deerskin on which he was lying.

"Rather be workin' out in de sun den layin' here wif dis cold creepin' into mah bones," grumbled Alfred. "Like t' freeze mah ass off."

"Dat's becuz Jeb Porter don' mess wiff you de way he does de rest of us," said Thornton. "He half scared a you."

"Huh! Scared a Massa Harness more like it," Augustus corrected him. "Alfred ain't about t' whup Jeb Porter long as he an' dat shotgun sharin' de same ho'se. But if Jeb Porter be shootin' Massa's bestes' slave he gwine have to answer to de man hisself."

"Don't have t' whup a man t' keep him off'n yo back,

'Gustus. I works hard an' keeps my mouf shut."

"You soun' lak you rather be back 'cross dat rivah sho 'nuff," replied Augustus, trying to sound out his taciturn older brother.

"Mama takin' a big risk fo you an' me, 'Gustus. 'Stead a jus' you an' me goin' down rivah, could be de whole fam'ly now."

"Mama say we ain't goin' down rivah, Alfred. None of us."

"Da's right, Thornton, tell 'im de way it be: we goin' clean t' Canady. We free now an' we gwine *stay* free!" exclaimed Augustus.

"Sho we is, not sayin' we ain't," Alfred hastened to reassure them. "But if you gwine be talkin' 'bout de '*way it be*,' 'Gustus, den let's look at it dat way. Thornton, dis be jus' 'mongst de men of de fam'ly, you heah? Don' be sayin' none a dis to Mama or Henry."

"Ah won'," said Thornton, proud to be included of course, but suddenly fearful of what he might be about to hear.

"You heard what Mizz Palmer done say: three weeks befo' we be safe in Canady. Dat's if'n we don't git caught or have to hunker down somewheres while dey lookin' fo us. Lots can happen in three weeks, 'Gustus. Best we *be* worried some's, de way I look at it. You an' me specially can't relax fo' a minute. We countin' on a whole lotta people, includin' *white* folks we don' know nothin' 'bout, t' he'p us 'long de way."

"Dey done right by us so far," pointed out Augustus.

"Sho dey has. I be right relieved – so far. Ah'm jus' sayin' we gots a long way t' go fo' we can start thinkin' 'bout bein' free an' *stayin'* free lak you say. An' even when we free, what den – what de hell *dat* mean? How long folks be hep'in' us? You knows I ain't skeered a hard work, but hard work gwine be nuff t' care fo Mama an' de fam'ly in a place we know nothin' about?"

"You talk lak we all jus' dependin' on *you*, Alfred, lak we cain't do nothin' on our own. Now dat we free, we *on* our own – dat's what free mean. We all gwine do our share. Ain't lak it all be on yo head alone."

The short discussion had given all three of the brothers something to think about, and nothing more was said for a few minutes until Augustus broke the silence again. "Me, ah'm gwine find me a rivah somewheres. Don' have t' be de one we just cross long as it's goin' somewhere else an' big enough t' float a steamboat I can work on."

"Why you like rivahs so much?" Thornton asked, daring to challenge his brother to hear him wax eloquently on his favorite subject.

"I jus' done tol' you, Thornton – cause it always be *goin'* somewhere. And now *I* be free t' go 'long wif it. Ain't nothin' lak a rivah fo leavin' a man's cares an' worries behind. Dat big ol' paddlewheel jus' be choppin' 'em up, choppin' 'em up and strewin' 'em in little bitty pieces in all dat white water trailin' behind. Yassuh, left behind. What be yo plans, li'l brothah?"

Delighted to be asked, Thornton had to think a moment before realizing he had none. "Ain't got no plans, 'Gustus. I just tryin' to do what y'awl an' Mama say."

Perhaps because he looked a little shame-faced at this admission, Augustus reached over and gripped his brother's slender leg affectionately. "Dat's de bestes' thing you can do right now, Thornton: what me an' Alfred an' Mama tells you. You lucky you a kid, you know dat? You has purt' near yo whole life t' be free."

Outside the cave Nate Lucas, Jewett Palmer's hired hand, jumped the shallow creek and climbed partway up its rocky bank before kneeling at the nearly invisible entrance to the cave where Jane's sons were hiding.

"You fellers ready fer some supper?"

This was good news to all of them.

"Ah bin ready since dem samwiches you brung," Augustus called out to him. "Seem like yestiddy, but dey was *good*."

"No one puts a better meal in front of a man than Mizz Palmer," agreed Lucas. "Bring them skins with you."

"We buried our scraps lak you said," Thornton, the first one out, told him. "Nobody gwine know we was here."

His brothers crawled out behind him, then stood up to stretch, taking deep breaths after a day spent essentially underground.

"Dat fresh air sho smell good," said Alfred.

"*Food* what ah'm needin', brother – le's git movin'," urged Augustus.

"Where's Mama?" Thornton asked the hired hand.

"Mr. Palmer's gittin' her and your sisters. Follow me now – remember, quiet as you can."

As night fell over Marietta, a group of Harness's riders had settled in at Injun Island, one of the rowdier taverns on the levee. Attended by friendly bar girls who kept the beer and liquor flowing, to the sound of an off-key piano to which no one was listening anyway, they were playing an alcohol-addled, not particularly high-stakes game of poker in the crowded, smoke-filled bar.

Outside on Ohio Street, carousers weaved and stumbled under gas lamps down the treacherous wooden sidewalks. While in a tawdry room at Big May's, James Lee Forrester lay in bed with the curvaceous Creole named Orleanna, whose fragile beauty was so deep, or distant, no man could fathom it.

"Baby, it gets better every time I see you."

"You should come more often," she drawled.

"You're too damned expensive. If we don't catch them slaves, I'll be broke till next payday."

The young Virginian was blissfully unaware when Orleanna's sultry manner suddenly cooled a few degrees. "I wondered if that's why you was in town."

"Runaway slaves and you, Baby's, the only things I come to Ohiah for. Too many free niggers and abolitionists over here."

"Why you wanta be houndin' some poor old woman and her kids? Ain't you got nothin' better t' do?"

"Sure, Honey," he said, moving against her – "this is a *whole* lot better."

"Better'n chasin' women and children all over the countryside? That sounds like a lotta fun t' me."

"Why the hell do you care anyway?" asked the Virginian in annoyance. "You ain't no slave woman."

"...Thank God for that," she murmured.

"Well the one we're after is – goddamn runaway slave. And them 'kids' as you call 'em are grown men and women, some of 'em. And they belong to Solomon Harness."

"Hey, Sugar," said Orleanna, softening her tone of voice, "why you gettin' so hot an' bothered?"

"Cuz you're makin' a big fuss outa somethin' you don't know the first thing about. I sure didn't come here for that."

Orleanna's eyes no longer complemented her bedroom smile; there was anger verging on hatred in them. But the handsome young Virginian was oblivious to it.

"...I know what you come for, Sugar. Jus' teasin' you is all. You get rid a them angry thoughts now, and let's have us some fun. Okay?"

"...Yeah. That's more like it."

"We gonna have us a little fun, you and me," said Orleanna – good, but really having to work at it right now.

9

I never ate so good before that first meal on the underground railroad. I wakes up stiff and hungry and the big basket of food Mizz Palmer had for us done fill me up for the first time I can remember, always hungry when I a slave. Even when we have a lot of food in the summer from the garden, corn and greens and melons and such, seems like it never enough, especially when I starts carrying a baby.

I figure we be hiding out there in the barn and after eating my fill I'm ready to lay down in that nice soft hay, but Mr. Palmer say its not safe, they have to separate the family. He don't say why but I figure its so if Master Harness or a bounty hunter catch some of us he don't catch all of us and I starts into worrying again. But they puts Mama and me together and we gets to talking like we hardly ever done back on the slave side of the river.

We crawl in amongst this thick stand of pine trees and I be feared of snakes but we don't see any. Its shady and cool in there and theres a little breeze sighing through the branches. Somehow I gets to thinking about James again and starts snuffling a little but trying not to cry and worry Mama. I know she knows though cause she starts talking about my baby and how glad she be its gone grow up free. When you a real mama like me she says you know what I mean. She puts her hand real gentle on my belly which just now starting to swell a little and now I do cry cause Mama hardly ever done touch me like that before except when I'm sick and I hardly ever be sick. Mama always be working too hard, too tired and too sad to touch any of we children seems like. So I hug her again like last night in the wagon, then she start crying too and soon we both be bawling like a couple of calves.

You really think we gone make it Mama I say after a while and she gets that look where her eyes be hard and you know she done made up her mind to do something no matter what. We'll make it she says. You think James will find us? If he wants you and his baby bad enough he will she says. His old mama won't live forever, then we see what kind of man he is and how he feel about being a daddy. Somehow I feel sure I'll never see James again but I don't tell Mama.

Then she start talking real slow and quiet about things she never told me before, about my own daddy. Rachel cried the hardest when they done took him away she said, couldn't get her to stop for two days. But I figure you hurt the most cause you never even make a sound, never say a word. Mama surprise me when she say that cause I never thought much of my daddy until I fell so hard for James. Sometimes I be holding James and he be kissing me and loving me and I get this strange feeling I be a little girl somehow, like it was something already happened long time ago.

I tell Mama this and she just nod her head and more tears run down her cheeks but she don't cry. Your daddy be a fine man Caroline she says, a strong man but a gentle man too. I look at him she says and look at Massa Harness and all the poor white trash that done work for him, I look at the fancy dressed riverboat man done took him away, and I ask myself how it be that the better man, the good strong gentle man that love his family be the one going down the river in chains and the no account men be free. Thats why we going to Canada Caroline she says. So your baby and all my grandchildren, if they be boys or girls don't matter, be able to live the lives they choose for themselves. She keep on talking like this for a long time and pretty soon I see how it don't matter if I be listening or not, its like shes telling herself these things, so I done fell asleep.

While their pursuers were carrying on in Marietta, the fugitive family began the second grueling night of travel on their clandestine journey north, to the Markey Station in Noble County. If successful, the improvisational zigzag from station to station at the discretion of their conductors would land them eventually on the southern shore of Lake Erie: a steamboat's passage from Canada and freedom.

Still bothered by her nagging cough and the wagon's rough ride, Jane was again unable to sleep. Fear for her children's safety had roused her from the lifelong depression with which slavery held the heart in chains. And this enforced idleness which she'd never experienced before, even in sickness and childbirth – sleeping by day, or trying to, and lying awake at night on a hard, jolting wagon bed beneath the stifling canvas cover which at once shielded and suffocated Jane and her daughters – gave her too much time to remember and to grieve. Long dulled by time and familiarity, the old anguish of loss – of mother, brother and husband – had been awakened in her family's flight through these dark sultry August nights.

She could remember as if it were yesterday the day Tom ran, 20 years ago. An overseer even worse than Jeb Porter – Roy Akins was his name – had been bothering her for days, by turns cajoling and threatening her just to get her down in the hay for a few minutes to relieve the itch of desire. She hadn't dared tell her husband. Justin would have gone for the man and surely died for it, whether Akins killed him or Harness did over his overseer's dead body.

If only it could have been the one time, she might have relented. But of course it wouldn't be just once; it would be again and again until he'd finally slaked his lust and obsession and tired of her. So she had resisted him, using all the wiles of which she and Hannah were possessed to avoid being caught alone in his presence.

But the day Tom ran, and Jane was crippled forever, Akins had lain in wait for her at the stable. She'd come in carrying water for Harness's stallion – several horses before the big bay he rode now. Akins had caught her unawares, her arms effectively pinioned for a moment by the heavy bucket in each hand – too heavy to swing at him as weapons. He'd dragged her into an empty stall beside the coal-black Morgan, which became increasingly wild as Jane struggled with her attacker.

She screamed once before Akins clamped his hand over her mouth then slammed her down on her back in the straw and began to rip at her clothes.

"Quit fightin', you black bitch!" he snarled like some maddened ferocious cur, spewing spit; his fetid breath, the awful unwashed smell of the man almost overpowering in itself. "You been askin' fer this!"

Jane bit his hand and when he roared in rage and pulled it away she screamed again. That's when Tom found them. He came running in with the pitchfork he'd been using in the barn, straw or hay still caught in the tines.

She remembered crying out, sobbing his name in grateful desperation, but Tom hadn't said a word. He moved in with the pitchfork, then thought better of using it for fear of hurting his sister. Throwing it aside, he lunged at the overseer – who had pushed her away to defend himself. Akins was a wily fighter, but Tom was much the stronger of the two. He was soon beating the man mercilessly – until the would-be rapist managed to grab the pitchfork.

Feinting with it but unable to zero in on his opponent, who kept frantically dodging and ducking, Akins finally saw his chance when Tom slipped in the loose hay. But when the overseer rushed him Tom rolled away at the last instant, and the tines of the pitchfork ripped through the wooden slats of the stall into one of the stallion's hind legs. Screaming in pain, the big horse smashed the side of the stall, and Jane's left leg, with one ferocious kick.

...That night in her cabin, after Tom had beaten the overseer so badly he'd never been able to work for Harness again, then vanished into the woods with nothing but the torn and bloody clothes on his back, Hannah had cleaned and set the mangled leg as best she could. Furious at losing both his overseer and a prime field hand, Harness hadn't even told the doctor attending Akins that a slave had also been injured.

In her delirium, often sobbing uncontrollably, Jane had asked again and again: "But *why*, Mama? When all he doin's tryin' t' pull that man offa me?"

"Jane, Jane – I don't say it's *right*, chile! God knows it ain't *right*," Hannah patiently explained each time her daughter repeated the question. "It's de way it *is*. Tom lucky t' git away."

"*Lucky*? How he swim all de way 'cross dat rivah? He drown fo sho."

"You bin outen yo head, gal. You keeps sayin' Tom done drowned hisself, an' ah keeps tellin' you some boy from de Box Plantation done *rowed* him 'cross in his boat. He be on his way to Canada now, Lawd willin'....You res' yose'f now. Tom say he git word t' we when he safe."

But he never had. After all these years would her family's flight to Canada unite Jane with Tom again as well as gaining their freedom?

10

The next morning Harness was finishing his breakfast in the hotel dining room when his disheveled-looking overseer sat down at the table opposite him.

"They ready?"

"Some of 'em may fall asleep in the saddle," said Porter, "but they're ready. Where we headed?"

"Place called Middleburg, north of here. The Severance farm."

"That's abolitionist country all right."

"Runaways was seen on the Severance farm a month ago. These could be that far by now."

At the livery stable, hung-over, surly and ill-kempt, the Virginians were not a happy posse this morning as they choked down – or avoided – the hard dry cornbread Harness had provided for breakfast, while saddling their horses.

"I'll bet Harness feeds his hounds better'n this," grumbled the dashing young Forrester.

"What's wrong, son? Your 'honey' go sour on ya?" needled Seevers, the senior rider among them.

"Hell yes she did!" said another. "He come sneakin' in here about three o'clock this morning."

"Ah, they're all niggers underneath," snarled Forrester.

"Coffee's coffee, I always say," Seevers philosophized, "no matter how much damn cream you put in it."

Riding north out of town soon afterwards, with

Harness in front on his magnificent bay, the Virginians took up the full width of the dirt street. On the outskirts they were approached by Jeb Coursey, beginning the day's rounds of collecting horse droppings in his wagon.

"*Whee-ew*! What the *hell* is that *smell*?" someone taunted him.

"Get them damn mules outa the way!" commanded Harness.

Coursey was already pulling as close to the side of the road as possible.

"Goddamn niggers this side a the river think they can do anything they please!" ranted Porter, loud enough for the elderly driver to hear. Coursey waited till they were safely past, then whipped his mules into a vigorous trot toward the home of David Putnam, Jr., in Harmar, across the river from Marietta on the west bank of the Muskingum.

Born in Harmar in 1808, Putnam had come of age at the right time in American history, in a strategically crucial location and with the requisite upbringing and education, to become a leader of the Underground Railroad. The great-grandson of General Israel Putnam, a farmer who left his plow to fight in the battles of Lexington and Concord at the beginning of the American Revolution, Putnam was also a cousin of Brigadier General Rufus Putnam, Revolutionary War veteran and leader of the Ohio Company, which founded Marietta in 1788.

David Putnam, Jr., began his fight against slavery as a teenager after becoming personally acquainted with a number of the 800 or so slaves in Wood County at the time and listening to their fears of being sold down the river. Now a merchant in good standing in Marietta, Putnam and his wife Hannah were raising a family of seven children, amidst his not-so-secret activities with the Underground Railroad, in a stately 14-room home on two acres at the head of a shady brick street lined with maple trees.

A tall muscular fellow equally comfortable settling disputes with diplomacy or his fists as the situation required, Putnam had many supporters willing to come to his defense, even though the abolitionist movement was almost as unpopular in southeast Ohio as the idea of slavery itself. To most residents, the Washington County Anti-Slavery Society, founded in 1836, and the area's 50 or so anonymous conductors and stationmasters on the Underground Railroad were troublemakers bringing unrest to a peaceable community. Though against slavery themselves, they had come to accept its existence on the Virginia side of the river as an unpleasant, occasionally even convenient, fact of life. It was not unusual, for example, for farmers and tradesmen to rent or borrow slaves during the harvest season or when their workload was heavier than normal.

The Putnam house had been surrounded on several occasions by unruly citizens, not all of them Virginians, looking for runaway slaves. Most in the crowds were the angry, unsuccessful people, from both sides of the river, who make up any mob; they despised Putnam as much for his principles and fine house as they did for his flouting of the law. Although the Fugitive Slave Law of 1793 didn't require the citizens of free states to assist slaveholders in capturing runaway slaves, it clearly forbade the clandestine activities of the Underground Railroad.

In fact, because of the constant scrutiny both it and he received in the community, Putnam sheltered fugitives in his home only under the direst circumstances. Such was the case one dreary November night when Hannah lay in labor with the Putnams' sixth child. Her husband had already gone for the doctor when an angry crowd began to gather, punctuating anti-abolitionist epithets with stones thrown against the sides of the house. A runaway slave had been tracked to the Virginia side of the Ohio River, and the consensus of the bi-state congregation below was that the Putnam home was the obvious place to search first. It was almost midnight when Putnam finally returned with Dr. John McCoy and three leading Washington County businessmen, whose task was to keep the crowd from breaking in the Putnams' door and ransacking the house. One of the men was Col. Augustus Stone, a prominent landowner and the son of Col. John Stone, the founder of Belpre, Ohio, and stationmaster on the Underground Railroad in that community.

McCoy, a self-assured, physically imposing man, was a prominent figure in the community, often seen striding through his rounds protected against the weather by a flowing black cape and high-crowned black hat tilted over his face in a manner at once rakish and vaguely sinister. The torch-bearing crowd parted respectfully to let the doctor through but yielded with less tolerance for the three would-be peacemakers who began to circulate amongst them with pleas for restraint and common sense.

"For God's sake," exclaimed Col. Stone. "Mrs. Putnam's about to give birth inside! Show the family some common decency!"

But a cold rain which had begun to fall only intensified the sullen mood of the assembly. Although no one had thought to obtain a search warrant and none of the vigilantes as yet dared to be the instigator of an illegal, possibly tragic trespass, the tension had become extreme when McCoy's departure an hour or so past midnight seemed to break the spell.

"The Doc's leavin', I'm goin' too!" called out one of the wet, miserable men in the crowd. One after another of the ruffians followed his example until only a few of the most ardent abolitionist-haters remained when, at daybreak, the *real* McCoy emerged, unrecognized for a moment because of the absence of his well-known top hat and cloak. This wasn't the only instance – just the most dramatic – in which a fugitive slave seeking refuge in the Putnams' home had used a disguise and the cover of night to slip safely through a hostile crowd.

Putnam took his life in his hands every time he crossed the Ohio. A few years before, he had nearly drowned when driven to the wharf and into the river by an angry mob in Parkersburg, Virginia, some 12 miles south of Marietta. He owed his survival to his strong stroke and the fortuitous presence of a Marietta-bound sternwheeler whose deckhands pulled him aboard. Though not all of Putnam's disputes with slaveholders were life-threatening, some had taken a lot longer to resolve, such as a four-year legal battle with the owner of the Henderson plantation. Henderson had claimed – no doubt correctly in this case though some would have liked to see Putnam implicated in the disappearance of every slave from Wheeling to Cincinnati – that he had aided in the escape of nine of Henderson's slaves.

...Standing now on his front porch with Jeb Coursey, Putnam thanked the free black man for his information and promised to alert station managers to the north that Harness and his posse were on their way.

"Ah sho hopes he don' ketch 'em," said Coursey, frowning.

"He won't, Jeb." Putnam gripped his hand gratefully, prompting a glow of pride on the old man's deeply lined face.

The Rev. Joseph Markey, a tough-minded, large-hearted conductor on the Underground Railroad, stood beside the spotted Indian pony on which his son Jonas was mounted at their Noble County farm. Jonas was a lean, good-looking, deeply tanned youth of 17. Between them they ran the Markey Station, where Jane's family had arrived from the Palmers' last night.

"Ride to the Severance farm and let 'em know our passengers should be in Summerfield tomorrow morning," Markey said to his attentive son. "Tell Severance they seem to be in pretty good shape – the mother's comin' down with a cough, is all." He slapped the horse's flank, and Jonas cantered out of the farmyard to the road.

Having to cover only about four miles, young Markey was in no hurry. He sat back in the saddle, enjoying the coolness of the woods and his pony's easy ground-covering gait. The narrow, generally level wagon trail wound through virgin hardwood timber broken by the occasional farmstead surrounded by a few acres of cleared land, much of it planted in corn and tobacco. As he had been eagerly anticipating, he arrived at the Severances' just in time for the noon meal.

"By God, he done it again," cried one of the farmhands on their way up to the house to eat – "got here just in time fer dinner!"

"You think this ol' farmboy can't tell time?" laughed Jonas before watering and tethering his horse.

In the dining room he was greeted enthusiastically by Wilhemina Severance, an attractive woman of generous proportions whose family was part of the large German contingent in southeast Ohio. Her meals were always ample.

"Chonas Markey! Chust in time for *wurst* and *apfelstrudel*. Can I get you a glass of cider?"

"Thank you, Mizz Severance, that sure would be welcome. It's hot out there this morning."

He returned her big hug with affection, then spotted the Severances' eldest daughter Mathilda, a shy teenager recognized by the family's many friends and acquaintances as the spittin' image of her mother. With her younger sister

Gretchen, she was helping to serve the dozen or so men seated at the long table, heavily laden with tomatoes, sweet corn and fresh vegetables in addition to the German fare.

"How do, Mathilda."

"Sit down, Jonas," she replied, blushing and smiling sweetly. "Gretchen, get Jonas a plate."

Young Markey pulled an empty chair from the table, hung his sweat-stained hat on the back, and immediately took part in the passing of heaping plates of food. Philip Severance, a hard lean man with the sharp eyes of the gun-fighter he might have been had he grown up some 1,500 miles farther west, was the last to enter and be seated, at the head of the table.

"Howdy, Jonas. I expect you have some word from your father. We'll speak of it after dinner." He bowed his head, followed by the rest of the table. "Oh Lord, we thank Thee for this, the bounty of Thy love and generosity. May it give us strength to serve Thee and do Thy work. Amen."

The silence was broken as suddenly as it had descended, with the clamor of the hearty meal.

At a crossroads a few miles to the south, with dirt roads and wagon tracks heading off in several directions, Solomon Harness raised his arm, and the Virginians behind him reined in their horses. A wooden trail sign with the names of towns burned into arrows pointing in different directions lay on the ground.

"I don't figure that just fell over now, do you?" drawled Jeb Porter.

"Anyone remember the way to Middleburg?" asked Harness.

"To the right, Harness. 'Fore long your memory's gonna be as bad as mine," replied Seevers.

"He's right, Mr. Harness – 'bout the road, I mean," stammered a much younger rider.

Harness wasn't amused. He kicked the bay's wet flanks, and the posse galloped up the road to Middleburg.

The loft of the tobacco-drying shed on the Severance farm had been secretly converted for temporary habitation. Rose and Howard Neale, a fugitive slave couple in their mid- to late-20s, were currently sharing the cramped quarters with their newborn daughter, who was nursing at the moment. Dinner for the hired hands and large Severance family was over, and Wilhemina had just brought the Neales' meal to them.

"Thankee kindly, Mizz," said Howard, taking the tray full of food.

"Thank you, Ma'am," added his wife, "this look awful good."

"You chust enjoy that and then rest comfortable," said Wilhemina. "Ve be back to check on you."

"...No wonder she couldn't wait till we gets t' Canada," said Howard, gazing fondly at their nursing baby. "She too hungry."

Rose baby-talked her tiny daughter while her husband laid out their meal for them. "How long you think they let us stay?" she asked.

"Long as we needs to, they said."

"Her little face jus' look so precious – don't it, Howard?"

"She gwine be beautiful as her mama," he replied, caressing his wife's wan face. "You eat now yose'f, you needs to git yo energy up fo de rest of de trip."

11

In big wicker rockers Severance and Jonas Markey worked off the noon meal, ballast in their full bellies, in the shade of the wide front porch. A large hunting hound was sprawled on the floor as though dead between them. The cicadas, everywhere and nowhere, had started up again – neither could say just when – so that the hot afternoon seemed to pulsate in a rhythm the rockers themselves had unconsciously embraced. Jonas had just delivered his father's message while the two of them sat here digesting the heavy meal and Severance smoked his pipe.

"When did the Underground Railroad get its start, Mr. Severance?" asked his well-fed visitor. "Have you and my father and the others around here been involved in it from the very beginning?"

"Well, I doubt that anyone rightly knows for sure, Jonas," replied Severance, pulling on his pipe and squinting thoughtfully. "Slaves have been runnin' off ever since there was slavery, and there was always some that helped 'em. Indians at first, then other slaves and free blacks. Folks like us get involved where there's no black family or community to hide runaways. But black folks themselves, like Cajoe Phillips over in Waterford, have always been the most active."

"I hear tell Cajoe's a hundred years old," said Jonas, scratching the dog's ears and stifling a yawn – not from a lack of interest but in response to the heat, the heavy meal and the relaxing rhythm of the rocker.

"He may be but he still runs the station he started up

over there."

"Like the black folks in Stafford and Guinea."

"That's right. And since there's no way a fugitive slave could make it all the way to Stafford from the Ohio River in one night, abolitionists stepped in to fill the gap, you might say. Course the name 'Underground *Railroad* ' didn't come along till the real thing did, back in the '20s and '30s. Someone must have thought the name fit because of the way runaways are passed along from station to station, and it just sorta stuck. But the movement itself, the secret network of people helpin' slaves escape, that began well before the railroads did. Not as early as some folks think though."

"What do you mean, Mr. Severance?" asked Jonas, aroused by the sudden scent of disputation in the air.

"Well, for one thing, there was no safe place for slaves to run to at first; there was slavery in every state."

"What about Canada?"

"Canada too. Canada didn't abolish slavery till 1793. And two other things happened that year that also had a strong bearing on the Underground Railroad."

"The Fugitive Slave Law?"

"That was one of 'em. Canada outlawing slavery gave fugitives a safe haven, and making it a crime here in this country to help them escape drove the whole thing to secrecy – 'underground,' in other words."

"What was the third thing?"

"The invention of the cotton gin." Jonas looked a bit confused, so Severance added: "You see, after the war of independence, slavery was actually beginning to die out. General Washington had promised to free slaves who fought in the Continental Army and, besides that, a hundred years of tobacco growing had depleted the soil to the point where it was no longer economical to farm in a lot of places."

"But we still grow tobacco around here," Jonas interrupted, becoming more animated the less he followed Severance's train of thought. "What's the cotton gin got to do with *tobacco* anyway?"

"I'm gettin' to that," said Severance, relighting his pipe with frustrating deliberation. "Eventually, we'll probably no longer grow tobacco here either. Even places like the Harness plantation with all that rich bottomland are going to have to look for some other crop. Tobacco's just too hard on the soil." He took a preliminary puff and, satisfied that his pipe was going to stay lit, continued: "...Meanwhile, back east some, what? 60 years ago, you had immigrants flooding into this victorious young nation of ours calling itself 'the land of the free,' and you had a lot of farmland that was no longer very fertile. So landowners began either selling it or building on it, turning it into houses, shops, factories. Either way, there was a growing surplus of slaves brought over here to clear swamps and plant tobacco with no real work for them to do any more. Not only was feedin' 'em expensive as hell, but think what they were doing to the labor market. Why pay some European immigrant to do what a slave could do for free?"

"So slaveholders set their slaves free just so they wouldn't have to feed them anymore?"

Severance chuckled. "That was one of the reasons – that and the labor situation and the fact that the Father of Our Country had promised to. One state after another began to abolish slavery, and some thought it was just a matter of time till the southern states did the same. *That's* where Eli Whitney came in. All of a sudden his cotton gin made it possible to clean 50 times as much cotton in a day as you could without it, and almost overnight cotton became the backbone of the South's economy. Which it is to this very day."

"Slaves were needed again, this time in the South."

"That's about the size of it, Jonas. If you want to pin a specific beginning on the Underground Railroad, I'm not sure you could come up with a better date than 1793. Unless it's 15 years later."

Seeing that he was being given an opportunity to redeem himself as far as American history was concerned, Markey, thoroughly awake now and stimulated by Severance's attention and their one-sided conversation, wrinkled his smooth young brow in concentration. "Don't tell me...1808...Oh *yeah* – that's when congress abolished the slave trade."

"Very good," acknowledged his teacher. "Not only were slaves needed again, but they could no longer be imported, which made them even more valuable. No more slave trading, legally anyway, between the United States and other countries, but still plenty of trade within our own boundaries, along with slave *breeding* to satisfy demand."

The boy's frown this time was from disgust rather than concentration. "I thought I knew a lot about slavery, but you make it sound even worse."

"Then now you have an even better grasp of why the Underground Railroad's so important," replied Severance. "Of course it took years for it to evolve into the organized movement it is now, up and down the Ohio River and in other states too. Although it may very well be right here in southeast Ohio where the Underground Railroad *as we know it today* got its start."

"That's what I asked you in the first place, Mr. Severance," said Jonas, a note of exasperation along with the admiration in his tone of voice. "How *did* it get started here?"

Severance had to pull the pipe from his mouth to accommodate his hearty laugh. "You've got as much persistence as you do spunk, Jonas," he said. "If you've got a few minutes I'll tell you the answer to that when I get back." He left the front porch with the dog behind him, and Jonas asked himself why a man as hard-working as Severance was taking the time to sit here and jaw with him. He was flattered but too smart to think there wasn't some other reason.

It be a lot harder getting in that wagon the second night than the night before when we wet and cold and scared Master Harness gone catch us any minute. We hates to leave Mizz Palmer's cooking and the peace and quiet of their nice little farm, lot different than the plantation even if we wasn't slaves there. It be a better night for traveling though, clear with no fog and a light warm breeze, neither too cool outside the cover when we stops to take a break nor too hot underneath it. Mamas started coughing since last night, all that wet and cold and her being so tired out all the time. I feel closer to her than ever I can remember after we done talk together there in the pines on the Palmer farm off and on all day. Strange having time for soulful conversation without we all being too tired or chores to do, something none of us be used to. Rachel say the same thing, how she and Fanny talk all day. Couldn't sleep much with the sun up. Me I sleeping for two Mama say but still time to talk and get to know things about Mama I never knew before, how she think about things, not just what happen to her. I ask her what Canada be like and she say she don't know much except it be cold and snow a lot and we be free. I sure knows what it ain't though Caroline she say. Ain't the way we been living all our lives. Anything be better than that even dying if its to change things, set our family free.

She start talking about Grammaw Hannah, how she not angry all the time like Mama cause she somehow know someday her kin and black folks everywhere be free. I tell Mama I didn't know she always angry, just tired and sad and quiet, mad when something go wrong especially when one of we children do something, but not all the time. Mama say she know she different from Grammaw Hannah, Grammaw say she an angry child, angry woman. Thats cause I don't see how me and my children ever be free Mama say. She think Grammaw's good humor just the way she is, make her believe things that ain't ever gone happen.

John be the first one done told Mama about the underground railroad. At first she don't believe no underground railroad gone save a woman with a family big as hers and no man around to help. Look at Tom she say, underground railroad sposed to help him but he never send any word he safe. Far as Mama know he be dead just like Justin. So how anyone expect her to run with seven children.

Then why you do it, Mama? Why you so sure now we gone make it safe to Canada I ask her. When they gone take my boys away like they done took my man I got no choice she say. Say she not sure till the very night we run that she gone do it. Then Grammaw speak to her beyond the grave. I see her plain as I seeing you Caroline she say, for just a heartbeat but clear as day. She tell me to run and not be afraid. My heart nearly stop right then she say but something change inside me. She still afraid and can't see how we gone make it but seeing Grammaw like that done make her see there be things in this world she know nothing about. If Grammaw Hannah tell her from beyond the grave just like she alive somewhere that we should run then maybe Hannah see what Mama can't.

I hug Mama then in that wagon because I see for all her telling us children we gone make it safe to Canada some part of her still ain't sure. Maybe its my own baby turning me day by day into a mama myself but I feel like comforting Mama like I'm the mother and she the child. I hardly ever felt this kind of love for Mama, maybe cause I never thought she need it nor I could give it to her. But now I see she more like me and

Rachel and the rest of us than I ever see before. And there be more sadness now in Mama, a look in her eyes I never done see there. It because I got too much time to think now she tell me, too many things to remember. And I know what she mean. I miss my man James something terrible sometimes and I just knows I'll never see him again. But can't turn my mind from sad thoughts with work or chores or even just a walk round the fields down by the river. I have to lay there in that wagon or lay round all day in some hidey hole like Mama and the rest and try not to think about it.

12

"Yessir, you're a chip off the old Markey grindstone, Jonas," said Severance when he'd returned with a glass of lemonade for each of them. "And that's appropriate since what may be the first Underground Railroad station the way it operates today is where most of the grindstones in this country are made."

"In Constitution, you mean?"

"That's right. Ephriam Cutler started the first Ohio station just south of Marietta in about 1810. And of course the old man's still very active, even though he must be close to 75 by now."

"I knew Judge Cutler was a stationmaster, but I didn't know he was the first," said Jonas, hoping Severance would continue the history lesson and give him an excuse to sit here in the shade of the Severances' balustraded porch a while longer. Like any local schoolboy who'd paid attention in class, Jonas knew many of the important details in the lives of both Cutler and his father Manasseh, author of Article 6 of the Ordinance of 1787, which prohibited slavery in the Northwest Territory.

"The first in Ohio anyway," replied Severance, sitting down with his lemonade in one hand and scratching his dog's head with the other. "Ephriam and his family left Connecticut in 1795 with three shares of stock in Ohio Company land and arrived in Marietta three months later. Most of 'em anyway; two of the Cutler children died of fever on the trip. Which should tell you that mosquitoes used to be a lot more dangerous in the Ohio Valley than hostile Indians ever were. Malaria, typhoid and yellow fever were all common causes of death here on the frontier then. The reason, along with river pirates, that many early settlers lived well away from rivers and streams."

"But not the Cutlers if they ended up on the Ohio River," Jonas pointed out.

"That's right – in fact before that, Cutler bought an 1,800-acre farm on the Muskingum, in Waterford, and built himself a mill. He wasn't afraid of rivers – or slavers either. His anti-slavery activities began in 1802, when he became the county's delegate to the Ohio Statehood Convention."

"Where he introduced a section of the state constitution excluding slavery in Ohio the way his father had for the whole Northwest Territory."

"You know your history, Jonas."

The young man grinned in spite of himself.

"But it could still have come to nothing, did you know that? If Cutler hadn't left his sickbed to cast the deciding vote, Ohio might be a slave state today."

"That's hard to imagine," said Jonas. "I couldn't stand livin' where people could own other people."

"Well, you can thank Ephriam Cutler and his father that you don't – and a lot of other folks too of course. By then Ephriam had extensive contacts among the Quakers and other abolitionists here in southeast Ohio, and after moving to Constitution he began to seek their help for fugitive slaves crossing the Ohio from Wood County, Virginia. By 1810 he and his friend John Stone, in Belpre, were conducting runaways along an Underground Railroad line that ran northwest from Constitution through the hills over to the James Lawson station in Barlow. Cutler, Ohio, was the next station, named for Cutler's son William – and before long you had stations spreading all through Ohio and into other states as well."

"...Are the folks in Guinea escaped slaves?" asked

Jonas, still holding the hot, humid afternoon at bay on Severance's broad front porch.

"One or two maybe, if they managed to get hold of some forged papers, or if they're just hidin' out for a while. But most of the people in Guinea are *free* blacks. Some may never have been slaves to begin with. Their ancestors may have been indentured servants – worked off their period of servitude till they'd earned their freedom, usually somewheres between seven and 14 years. Still others, slaveholders may have freed for one reason or another."

"For workin' hard, you mean – and bein' faithful and all?"

"Workin' hard?" Severance chuckled mirthlessly. "Hell, that's just taken for granted. Mules and slaves is why blacksnake whips come about, seems to me. Folks around here used t' think slavery would eventually be abolished, the way the British did in '34. But now it looks like it's here to stay – in our lifetimes anyway, mine and probably yours too, Jonas. No, the only time most slaves are set free, and it sure don't happen often, is generally after their masters die. They could never give 'em up while they was alive, but when they're about to meet their maker I guess some slavers have a change of heart. Not that their wishes are always honored," he added with a snort of contempt – "no matter what their will says. It's a bad business, Jonas."

"Yessir, I know it is," agreed Markey.

"I know you do, boy. I know your father always set you straight about that."

Suddenly Severance's dog growled and scrambled to its feet, the hair on its neck rising.

"What's wrong with Ulysses?"

"Riders," said Severance. "I expect that'll be Harness's men. Tell Mathilda to warn that young couple in the loft to keep their baby quiet – and get my shotgun from the cabinet."

So this was what had kept Mr. Severance hanging around the house – he'd been expecting Harness's posse all along! Jonas ducked inside while his host walked to the front of the porch, the now ferocious-looking dog at his side. The two of them made an imposing presence. Jonas returned a minute later and handed Severance his gun while Mathilda darted out the back door and ran unobserved toward the drying shed.

A hundred feet away, the riders stopped before a white picket fence surrounding the Severances' well-trimmed front lawn. Harness rode right up to the gate. In his dusty but well-tailored black suit, with steel-blue eyes and the air of one long accustomed to being obeyed he, too, cut a commanding figure. For a moment he sat aside his snorting lathered horse, looking around at as much of the farm as he could see.

"...Seen any niggers about?" he asked finally.

The tension was interrupted by Wilhemina Severance bursting through the screen door with a tray of glasses and a pitcher.

"*Nein*," she sang out with forced gaiety. "Can I offer you and your men some nice cool cider?"

"No, Ma'am," said Harness coldly, not much caring for German abolitionists. "I'm trackin' some a my niggers that run off, and I heard you been hidin' slaves here. Believe we'll be searchin' the place."

"That won't be necessary," said Severance, cocking the shotgun. "Go inside, Wilhemina."

At the sound or motion of the gun's being cocked, the dog suddenly bounded off the porch, ran to the fence and, snarling viciously, leaped against the gate – spooking the horses. The Severances and young Markey were treated to a 10-second rodeo as Harness's riders struggled to stay astride the frightened rearing animals. Jonas had to struggle himself, to keep from laughing aloud.

Though he quickly regained control of the bay, Harness had lost the advantage. Like Caleb and Hershel the day before, he found himself looking down the barrel of Severance's 10-gauge.

"I'll say good day to you and your vigilantes now, Mr. Harness," said Severance, aiming the gun at the slave-holder's chest.

"...We'll be leavin' for now," Harness replied, lips stretched taut in his grim, weathered face. "But if I don't find them niggers by nightfall, I'll be back. And that goddamned dog'll be the first thing I shoot!"

He wheeled his horse around, and the Virginians galloped back down the road they had just come up, leaving a heavy pall of dust in their wake.

"Better go for reinforcements, Jonas."

"Yes *sir*, Mr. Severance!" replied Markey with admiration.

"Tell your dad he'd better not move his passengers tonight, unless it's just to get 'em a little fuhther from the house."

May 20, 1864

My Dearest Brother Thornton,

What an extraordinary difference a couple of weeks can make. A few days that seem like lifetimes ago my fellow soldiers of the 27th and I were wanting into battle in the worst way. Now that we've finally been granted our wish, I'm fighting just to get it all over and done with. I know this is why I joined up, to fight the rebs and help save Abe Lincoln's Union after he freed us slaves. But in the last two weeks I've seen enough men killed and torn to pieces to last the rest of my natural life, Thorn. First there was heavy fighting May 6th on the Orange and Fredericksburg plank road near a little town not much more than a tavern and a few houses known as Wilderness. The 27th was relegated as usual to guarding the supply trains along with a division of cavalry. The next day as if caught in a slow-moving but mighty flood, the army and the trains headed southeast toward a town called Spotsylvania, some 40 or 50 miles north of Richmond, our ultimate destination. Although with the rebs between us and their capital we are forced to advance in vast sweeping arcs rather than straight ahead. Maj. Gen. Burnside led two divisions of the Ninth Corps against the enemy with some success, but the Fourth wasn't one of them. The only action the 27th saw was in the switchyards. But all this was about to change, in a way most unexpected and more horrible than I could ever have imagined.

Another of those infernal southern "Jebs," this one General Jeb Stuart rather than Solomon Harness's vicious lackey Jeb Porter, had all the roads converging at Spotsylvania covered, and the rebs were dug in for a real fight. Well, Thorn, the two sides commenced to butchering each other to the point where even we "worthless" colored troops were finally called into action. And of course we acquitted ourselves commendably, as if there should remain any real question of that after last year's exploits of the 1st Kansas Colored and the 54th Massachusetts assault on Fort Wagner. If I digress it's to avoid having to describe the carnage of the combat I witnessed – and engaged in, brother! – at Spotsylvania. We kept storming the rebs' fortifications, impregnable breastworks of logs and fence rails and piled dirt from the trenches dug behind them, in wave after wave but were driven back again and again. In several places we occupied ground close enough to engage them in hand-to-hand slaughter, give and take, but all that killing did neither side the least bit of good. Where we couldn't get to the rebs with our bayonets we hauled in cannon and shot them point blank with shot, shell and double charges of canister till the ramparts were riddled with human flesh and blood. Trees two feet thick were blown to splinters. Much of the time it was raining, and in the occasional silences of the artillery what you heard along with the rain and the ghastly sighing of the wind were the screams and shrieks and wild abandon of men being murdered, butchered, going crazy with blood lust – myself among them.

It didn't start out that way. I wasn't reluctant to fire my musket, but when I found myself face to face with the rebs with only that barricade between us, I hesitated for just a moment at the thought of thrusting cold steel between those logs and rails into human flesh, into another human being on the other side, reb, white or blue. But I didn't vacillate for long, I knew that to falter now would likely be fatal. And besides, there was such overpowering momentum and pressure behind me, all around me, to throw myself into the fight completely. Suddenly everything went red, like a fire blazing up in my head. I quite simply lost my mind, Thorn, surrendered to some savage part of myself I didn't even know existed. All at once I was plunging my bayonet into Jeb Porter, into Solomon Harness and the coward who tried to rape Mama, the slave traders who dragged our brothers' father down the river from his family. I stuck those damn rebs, Thorn, stabbed them, took their lives the way they stole ours. We all did there in the rain and the screaming and the din of the cannons until finally I was exhausted and alive in a quiet the likes of which I have never heard before. The quiet of the grave among the living, the wounded and the dead.

I can't write anymore, Thorn, even though I can't get those sounds and awful pictures out of my mind. Thinking of how glad I am that you will never have to see any of this, I remain,

your devoted brother,

Henry

13

With his son and others riding from farm to farm to enlist support in a possible confrontation between abolitionists and Harness's posse at the Severance farm come nightfall, the Rev. Joseph Markey lifted a trapdoor to rouse Jane's sleeping family.

"You folks best be up and about," he called out to them in the hot, airless twilit gloom of the drying shed loft.

"...How soon we be on the road?" asked Jane hoarsely.

"You're not goin' tonight – Harness has a posse in the area. After supper we're gonna scatter you round the farm."

Sleep fled instantly.

"I knew we shouldn't a run!"

"Shet yo mouf, Car'line! He ain't gwine find us," declared Alfred.

"Not if you'll do as we ask of you," agreed Markey. "The Missus will have supper out in just a few minutes." One by one while awaiting their meal, the fugitives stole down the ladder to a hidden chamber off the drying shed. This was the Markey Station's privy for Underground Railroad passengers, its existence well hidden not only by a secret doorway but by the strong pungent aroma of drying tobacco. Supper was passed around in the loft soon afterwards.

"Sho glad we don' hafta spend the night in that damn wagon," said Rachel, eliciting a frown of disapproval from her mother.

"That wagon's what's gwine git us t' Canada."

"You can always git out an' walk," suggested Alfred.

"Well, *I* cain't," said Caroline. "An' all that bouncin' aroun' cain't be doin' mah baby no good neither."

"Lak Mama said: better'n growin' up a slave, ain't it?"

"Min' yo mouf, Henry!"

"Henry's right, Car'line!" Augustus rebuked her.

"*Chirren*! Stop dis feudin' and fussin'!" pleaded Jane in a weak voice, holding her chest when she was overcome by a fit of coughing.

Alfred spoke up for her. "Listen to Mama! We nevah gwine git to Canada lessen we sticks t'*geddah*. Sho dis hard – hard on ever'body. Walkin' or ridin' all night, sleepin' all day; Massa Harness after us....But we done cross de rivah, an' dere ain't no turnin' back now. Looky here," he said, gesturing at their hearty meal of sausage, egg noodles and fresh vegetables: "We gots people he'pin' us we don't even know. Folks takin' a big risk fo we. Leas' we kin do is ack lak we grateful an' willin' t' do our part."

Alfred's intercession appeared to have restored peace for the moment; his siblings wore the shamefaced looks of the justly censured. After the meal had been cleared away, Jane and her daughters were led by Markey to a small cave a quarter of a mile or more from the house. Jonas took her sons to a heavily wooded part of the farm where several large trees had been felled earlier in the summer by a freak windstorm some claimed to have been a tornado. The virgin timber, which would eventually be cut into lumber, made an excellent hiding place.

Dusk saw the gathering at the Severances' of some 20 or so armed men riding in from all directions on horseback and in wagons and carriages from the isolated farms, hamlets and villages of Washington County. Traveling in David Putnam, Jr.'s, coach were the three civic leaders who had come to his aid the November night his sixth child was born. Although 63, Caleb Emerson, lawyer, former prosecuting attorney and onetime editor of the *Marietta Gazette*, still wrote on emancipation issues for journals in America and abroad. "Wouldn't miss a chance to lock horns with Harness," he told the others. "He's not about to put a woman and her children in chains on Ohio soil as long as I have anything to say about it."

"We're with you on that," agreed Harmar Mayor Courtland Shepherd (whose son would be killed two decades later in the Civil War). "Reckon I'll let you do the talking though; you have more of a way with words."

"Bet you'd like to have faced Harness in court wouldn't you, Caleb?" asked Augustus Stone, son of the Underground Railroad stationmaster in Belpre.

"My hands would have been tied by the damned Fugitive Slave Law," replied Emerson. "I'd rather take him on now that I'm a private citizen again – in court, or tonight if it comes to that."

Not far behind the Putnam party was a buggy driven by Rainbow's 47-year-old stationmaster Thomas Ridgeway. His much younger passenger was Marietta College librarian Samuel Hall, secretary of the Washington County Anti-Slavery Society and veteran of a number of confrontations between abolitionists and pro-slavery forces in the county. When he was Hall's age, Ridgeway had already been a British sailor, the survivor of a disastrous shipwreck, and an entrepreneur who had weathered the many difficulties of doing business on the Ohio frontier. He'd finally put down roots in a little community on the Muskingum River north of Marietta known as Rainbow, where he'd opened an Underground Railroad station.

Also heading north from Marietta was a wagon driven by barber Jerry Jones which carried three other free African-Americans: Jones's adopted son Daniel Strawder,

Jeb Coursey, and Tom Jerry, employed by a Marietta businessman suspected of belonging to a secret network of bounty hunters. As compelled by Ohio law and common sense, they each carried their freedom papers with them at all times. The $500 bond required of free people of color within 20 days of entering the state had probably been suspended or loaned to them by benefactors since none of them would likely have possessed such financial resources themselves. Jones and his passengers shared with all free, law-abiding people of color in Ohio the right to own property but not to vote, hold office, or serve in the military.

With hammer and chisel a year before, Strawder and Tom Jerry had rescued two slaves who'd managed, though chained together, to escape from an Ohio River sternwheeler and were hiding in reeds near the mouth of Duck Creek. Over the years, however, all four had been discreet enough in their Underground Railroad activities to have been privy to information proving vital at times in conducting fugitive slaves safely through Washington County.

But Jones had been adamant in convincing his companions to accompany him to the Severance farm tonight. "If them Virginians don't show up, no one's gonna think twice 'bout weuns bein' there," he argued after closing his busy alleyway barbershop off the Muskingum. "But iffen they do, we's gonna need all the hands we can round up."

The free blacks from Marietta weren't the only African-Americans traveling to Middleburg. Frank and Amos, the broad-shouldered sons of Basel Norman, one of some 5,000 African-Americans who'd fought in the American Revolution, were riding in by horseback from northern Washington County with the venerable Cajoe Phillips, Waterford's founding stationmaster. Coming from the western part of the county were white stationmasters Uriah Bailey from Bartlett and William Smith from Cutler, as well as a few determined men from mixed-race families in that community.

Everyone in Cutler knew of Smith's Underground Railroad activities, but his 5-year-old daughter's earnest explanation of what became of the many people passing "secretly" through their home seemed to have erased any controversy over the matter. "We just drop them in a big hole behind the barn," she told anyone who asked her to repeat the story, "and when they roll out the other end they're in Canada."

Local abolitionists' favorite anti-slavery story was one involving Col. Jonathan Stone, who was on his way to the Severance farm from Belpre with Daniel Goss and Thomas Hibbard in Hibbard's fast open carriage. Having earned his rank in the Ohio Militia, Stone had won with it the fear and animosity of Virginia slaveholders. When the state militia positioned a cannon on the riverbank aimed directly at Stone's home on the opposite shore, he knew he had to retaliate, but how? There were no cannons to be had in Washington County and the cost to have one shipped to Belpre would have been prohibitive.

But Stone was as resourceful as he was antagonistic to the idea of slavery. One morning the Virginians in Parkersburg awoke to find a cannon aimed right back at them from Col. Stone's front yard, and the militia was put on high alert. This antebellum brinkmanship might have escalated dangerously had a thunderstorm a few days after Stone's countermeasure not given away his ruse. Forced to brave the elements by their state of readiness, Stone's anxious and thoroughly drenched adversaries were astonished to witness the threatening cannon suddenly toppled by a gust of wind. The Virginians soon learned to their dismay that they had been threatened for days by a section of wooden drainpipe supported by a butter churn.

Some of the staunchest of the freedom fighters heading to Middleburg were Quakers, distinguishable by their conservative manner and attire. Fifty years earlier various groups of Quakers had trekked to the Northwest Territory, many from the South where their meeting houses had been sold to buy land in Ohio and to purchase the freedom of slaves at the Wheeling, Virginia, auction house. One group had settled in what was now Columbiana County, another to the south, across the Ohio from Wheeling at a place they named Mount Pleasant. Around 1804 Quakers from Mount Pleasant had purchased land in Morgan County and made their home around present-day Chesterhill, through which a branch of the Underground Railroad would soon run. Another group settled in Barnesville in Belmont County.

The determined men at Severance's farm represented numerous religious persuasions, including the Stafford stationmaster named, ironically, Church Tuttle, who had rejected Christian values entirely because he was unable to accept the fact that some Christians countenanced slavery as compatible with their faith. United in opposition, however, the congregation of abolitionists planned to forego sleep tonight, ready for trouble but prepared to enjoy the male camaraderie of standing up for what they believed in. A bonfire prepared by Severance's farm hands earlier in the day was ignited about midnight, partly for warmth, partly for illumination. The faces lit by the wavering glare of the flames were those of men certain of their cause and proud of their part in it.

"Pretty good turnout," remarked a cobbler who'd come all the way down from Sarahsville with his son-in-law. "I'd like t' see Harness and them hired guns a his take on this bunch."

"Let's hope it don't come t' that," replied Philip

Severance soberly.

"Don't look t' me like he's even gonna show up," said the owner of a sawmill near the community of Lebanon.

"Even if he don't," noted Severance with a sly smile, "he's gonna have t' figure, with all the men we got here, that this is where the passengers are."

Another group gathered around the bonfire included William Steel, the much respected head of the abolitionist movement in southeastern Ohio who ran the Stafford Station just a few miles northeast of here. Steel was a self-possessed Scottish immigrant with dark hair and piercing blue eyes which acquired all the hardness of his name when necessary.

"Harness must be losin' his touch, t' let a woman and a bunch a kids get away from him," said a short but heavily muscled man who was both blacksmith and horse doctor for the area.

"I hope to hell they *all* get away someday," growled the farmer who'd ridden in with him tonight.

Middleburg's secondary school teacher had surprised a number of the men just by showing up; few of them thought that he had the nerve. "Well, the British have outlawed slavery in all their colonies now," he pointed out. "Maybe the South will too."

"You're dreamin'!" the surly farmer contradicted him. "Not when their whole damn economy's *based* on slavery. They'll have to be forced t' do it."

"Who the hell's gonna force 'em?" someone else asked. "Slavery's like the plague: you're never gonna wipe it out. The best you can do is keep it from spreadin'."

"It *is* a plague – a moral one," Steel spoke up for the first time in a while, content as usual to listen and observe while others did most of the talking. "Slavery's as bad for *whites* in the South as it is for slaves. Poor whites think it's beneath them to work, and slaveholders become so corrupted by it – sleeping with their female slaves and then buying and selling their own children – that it's undermining their whole society."

"Ah, slaveholders will never face that," said the farmer again. "Not when all those black babies they're fathering just keep adding to their capital."

14

Though they hadn't walked all night like the men in the family, Jane and her daughters hadn't slept much in either the wagon or the drying shed during the day. The prospect of a good night's sleep instead of being crammed with her mother and sisters against another jolting wagon bed had seemed delicious to Fanny as the women in the family were led through the dark woods to a cave on the Markey farm in which she imagined herself being enfolded in the tender, mothering arms of oblivion.

The reality, however, was that Fanny and her sisters now lay awake on the cold hard ground, kept awake by their mother's periodic racking cough and the steady drip of water somewhere in the back of the cave. In being denied the release she had craved with an almost ravenous bodily hunger, Fanny felt frustrated enough to cry. But crying was an expression of emotion which she had all but forgotten in her young life. Instead, she tossed and turned on a rough woolen blanket on the damp floor of the cave, her eyes open yet seeing nothing but a sort of visual echo of those sleep-robbing sounds.

The others were all as sleepless and uncomfortable as Fanny, but for a long time no one spoke. Jane and the three sisters lay invisible from one another in the dark, contemplating not only the long hard journey ahead of them but the lives and people they'd left behind. Then all at once Rachel's clear thin voice startled the rest from their thoughts.

"Mama, tell us a story," she pleaded. "I cain't sleep and

I know y'all cain't neither."

"Tell us the one about the parrot at your old plantation," Caroline chimed in."

Although all her children considered Jane a good storyteller, with a sly sense of humor directed at the powerful, the posturing and the foolish, she certainly wasn't in the mood tonight for confabulatin', as Hanna, who had taught her the art, had called it. At least not in the fine points of atmosphere and characterization for which she was best know. But the parrot fable, one of her children's favorites and a tale that was at least partly true (which parts Jane was no longer sure of, so often had she embroidered and amended it over the years) was an easy one. She could tell that, even with a little feeling when she was feeling miserable, without having to think about it.

"...Well, as y'all know," she began, rolling onto her back, placing her arms beneath her head to stare up into the dark, "it was the custom where my mama and I used to live for the white folks to go to church on Sunday mawnin' and leave the cook in charge. And that 'ere cook, bless her heart, had a habit of bakin' cookies and handin' 'em out to the rest of us slaves before the massas returned. Now it jus' so happened one Sunday for some reason or t'other that the white folks got back sooner than we'uns expected, and the cook didn't have time to hand the cookies out. So she hid 'em in a drawer in a sewing chair.

"And I've told you 'bout the cantank'rous old parrot that allus sat on top of the door in this here room..." Even Fanny found herself being drawn in once again to the picture in her mind of that bright green parrot perched on a door in a room she'd never been in yet knew in elaborate detail. "Wellsuh, when the missus come in, that mean old bird commenced t' hollerin' out at the top of his voice: *They're in the rocker! They're in the rocker*!' The missus, she found the cookies and told the massa, and he called his man what done the whipping in and they tied up that poor cook and whupped her pretty good."

This was the part Fanny liked least about the story, but the cook's suffering was what made the parrot's fate so delicious. She imagined some brave male slave, whose face she had never quite been able to fill in, wringing its neck the way chickens on the Harness plantation met their maker for Sunday dinner. "The next morning," Jane concluded, "that 'ere parrot was found deader'n a doornail. Course another slave was accused of killin' it and they whupped him too – but after dat we nevah had no mo' spies wid wings round de place."

In the meantime some four miles to the southwest, as the cool summer night on the Severance farm deepened, its edge of excitement dulled by an uneventful passage of the hours beneath an unremarkable if nearly full moon, conversation had turned to the ordinary. Politics, the weather, prices of crops and livestock dutifully made the rounds.

"How's your corn crop this year, Severance?" asked Harvey Hovey, master of an Underground Railroad station near the hamlet of Lower Salem some five miles to the south.

"Corn crop's good. Gettin' it to market's the problem."

"You mean that boiler explosion on the Claire E?"

"On the Claire E, on the Ohio Belle, the Pride of Coshocton....If a body could build a boiler that wouldn't blow up, he'd make himself a rich man."

"You'll never catch me workin' on a Muskingum River steamboat," vowed young Jonas Markey, who had overheard the dialogue and found it more compelling than the fine points of planting times and crop yields. This led to a discussion of Ohio's recently completed "slack water" navigation system of locks, dams and a thousand-mile network of canals which had made the Muskingum River navigable for steamboats and connected the Ohio River to Lake Erie. The combination of natural and manmade waterways not only provided farmers and merchants with an expanded transportation system, but offered fugitive slaves yet another route to Canada, as stowaways. Inevitably, the conversation swung back around to success and horror stories connected with the Underground Railroad's newest line, and before long the abolitionists were sharing the worst of the accounts of slavery they'd heard from those fleeing the "peculiar institution."

"Sam, tell us some of the godawful things that's been told to you," Severance asked Samuel Hall, the college librarian. The passionate abolitionist had written many letters to the Anti-Slavery Society's national newsletter "American Slavery As It Is: Testimony of a Thousand Witnesses" describing incidents reported to him by local residents who had lived or traveled south of the Mason-Dixon Line. But Hall was not just a passive recorder of events.

At an anti-slavery meeting at the Harmar schoolhouse one cold February night eight years before, when he was still a college student, Hall had held a mob of Virginians armed with clubs, tar pots and sacks of feathers at bay with a pistol. "We're gonna give you goddamn abolitionists a memorable anointing!" someone in the crowd had yelled, and then the rest took up the chant: "Anoint the abolitionists! Anoint the abolitionists!"

But when no one was willing to take on the tall fiery-eyed man with a gun, the other members managed to escape through windows in the rear of the building. Then, stuffing the rusty, unloaded gun in his pocket and shielding his face with his heavy winter coat, Hall had dived through a side window and sprinted for the nearby Muskingum. With his long thin arms knifing through the frigid water, the young firebrand struck out for Marietta on the eastern side of the river, the enraged Virginians' curses ringing in his ears.

Now, with his craggy good looks and accusing, tragic eyes further dramatized by the flickering red light of the bonfire, Hall was more than ready to comply with Severance's request. Clearing his throat, he paused to collect his thoughts. "Well, gentlemen, I'm sorry to say I've heard hundreds of stories that would make any of you weep. It's hard to pick one in particular that's worse than the rest, but one atrocity that comes readily to mind was related to me by Isaac Knapp with whom I am well acquainted. He was a student at Marietta College for a year before going to Alabama and is now a professor of religion here – as worthy of belief as any member of the community.

"Prof. Knapp told me that in January of 1838 a runaway slave belonging to a woman named Mrs. Phillips – in a place called Upper Elkton, Tennessee, as I recall – was captured and put in jail some 15 miles away. Mrs. Phillips's overseer took the man from confinement and, mounted on horseback, compelled him to run all the way back to Elkton, whipping him the whole time. When he reached home exhausted and worn out, the Negro cried out, "You have broke my heart!" meaning in other words, "You have about killed me!"

For this the overseer flew into a violent passion, tied the man to a stake, and in the words of a witness 'cut his back to mincemeat.' But the fiend was not satisfied with this, gentlemen. He forced other slaves to burn the Negro's legs to a blister with hot embers and then chained him naked in the open air. It was a cold night, and in the morning the man was dead."

Hall stopped speaking and a murmur of outrage and disgust competed with the crackling fire to fill the silence his account had created among his listeners.

"Yet this monster escaped without even the shadow of a trial, gentlemen. A doctor said he didn't know how the Negro had died but in any case the overseer hadn't killed him."

"Well of course he got away with it!" shouted one of the now sullen men around the fire. "Nothing unusual about a slaver killin' a slave!"

"No," Hall agreed, "but in this case divine retribution may have intervened where man's justice failed. Later that year the overseer whipped another Negro unmercifully because the horse the slave was plowing with broke his reins and ran off. This time Mrs. Phillips's son – who had tried to have the man brought to justice for the earlier killing but was overruled by his mother – stepped in. And when the overseer raised his whip against *him*, the son shot him dead."

At this unexpected outcome, Hall's story was greeted with applause and coarse laughter. "Tell us another one!" shouted Jeb Coursey, "'bout how the Good Lord sets one slaver agin t'other!"

Hall's own somber demeanor was unchanged. "Well, as you all know, not many of the reports that come to us end the way that one did. Most of them are more like one Jim Glidden passed on to me. In the fall of 1837, Mr. Glidden shipped a boatload of produce down the Ohio and Mississippi where he witnessed an incident at a place called Matthews Bend, I forget in what state. He said he saw a Negro tied up and flogged until the blood ran down his legs; when he raised either foot and set it down the blood actually ran over the tops of his shoes. Well, Mr. Glidden told me he couldn't look on any longer and turned away in horror, while the whipping continued -- to a total of 500 lashes."

Even these seasoned men were taken aback by such a

figure. Hall had to raise his voice over muttered oaths and exclamations. "But that wasn't the end of it! A quart of spirits of turpentine was then applied to the Negro's lacerated body."

Now Hall was shouting to be heard: "Glidden said the man came down to his boat soon afterwards and was so weak from his wounds and loss of blood he couldn't get up the bank but fell to the ground and lay there. And the crime for which this Negro was whipped and treated this way, gentlemen? Mr. Glidden said it was for telling other slaves that the overseer had lain with his wife."

It had been apparent for some time that Harness's posse would make no appearance here tonight. But this litany of barbaric cruelty gave those among the abolitionists who were spoiling for a fight an opportunity to take on the Virginians *in absentia* at least.

"One thing the slavers do that sticks in my craw," offered James Lawton, founder of an Underground Railroad station in Barlow, several miles southeast of the Severance farm, "is the heartless way they herd slaves from place t' place like common cattle."

"Worse than cattle!" yelled another. "No man would be fool enough to do livestock the way slaves is treated!"

"Let me tell you fellows what a member of my congregation told me a few months back," said the Presbyterian minister who'd been in court the day before to learn the fate of the two slaves Harness had captured. "The young man shall remain nameless since he's from western Virginia, and I fear the consequences on his return if it were ever learned he had spoken out. He's an older student at the college, and I assure you his character and veracity are above suspicion.

"He told me that on the night of the great meteor shower ten years ago he was staying at a tavern outside of Lewisburg in Greenbrier County. Slave drivers with a drove of 50 to 60 Negroes headed south, chained together in groups of six or eight, stopped at the same place that night. The slaves usually camped out but as it was excessively muddy, they were permitted to come inside for a change. My parishioner said their supper that night was a compound of potatoes and meal, without exception the dirtiest, blackest-looking mess he had ever seen, worse in appearance than food given to a drove of hogs the same place the night before. Such as it was, however, a black woman carried it in on her head in a trough some two or three feet long, and the famished slaves rushed up and seized it in handfuls before the woman could set it down.

"That night they slept on the floor, lying in every form imaginable, males and females promiscuously. There were three drivers; one of them stayed in the room to watch the slaves; and the others each took a female from the drove to lodge with them in an adjoining room, as is the common practice of the drivers. The next morning the mud was so thick on the floor where the Negroes had slept it was necessary to use a shovel to clear it out."

"Hell, that's nothing," another man broke in. "I used to travel a lot in Virginia, and I've seen a dozen droves like that if I've seen a one. All going south. The winter the reverend was talking about, one bitter cold morning, I saw a drove of upwards of a hundred slaves, 40 or 50 of them fastened to one chain, with links made of iron rods thick as a man's little finger. They was headed west out of Clarksburg to the Ohio River. Ragged, nearly destitute of clothing, every one of 'em. Looked like they was half frozen. One little boy in particular excited my sympathy. He was some distance behind the others, unable to keep up, shivering from the cold and just a cryin' – the driver pushing him to a trot to overtake the main gang. Saddest thing I ever seen."

"Amen," said someone in a low voice audible only

because silence had again descended around the fire.

"Iron collars is another thing," volunteered Tom Ridgeway, as much to break the spell of melancholy as to express his personal antipathies toward slavery. "Some of the damnedest-looking torture contraptions a man could dream up. In Richmond I saw a colored woman, of intelligent and dignified appearance, attending the business of the house with a collar around her neck with prongs sticking out of it that came together a foot above her head, where there was a bell attached. A 'yoke' they called it, but it was a hell of a lot worse than anything you'd ever put on livestock. Just to keep the poor woman from runnin' away."

"Don't have to be around a man's neck to drive him crazy," added the sawmill owner from Lebanon. "I was down in Tennessee looking at a new mill a year or two back and they had slaves out logging in the woods. Hell, one poor devil had an iron fetter around his ankles, and how the dejected, heart-broke creature kept from gettin' hisself killed I'll never know. To keep the infernal thing from wearing his ankles when he walked, he held it up with a rope in one hand while he carried whatever he had to carry with the other. Whenever he had to lift the end of a log with both hands or lost his balance, which I saw him do a good many times, the torture of that damn fetter round his ankle, raw clean t' the bone, like t' done him in."

The fire burned lower now; the chill humid air was saturated with the smell of wood smoke. All the gallons of coffee and cider consumed throughout the night, along with a liberal indulgence in peach brandy among certain members of the entourage, were insufficient to hold back the encroachment of sleepiness and fatigue. With farm animals to feed, cows to milk and businesses to run, several of the men had already left. The consensus among those remaining was that Harness's threat had been mere bluster, he'd never intended to come in the first place.

"It's not just Harness they need t' worry about though." This from the owner of 180 prosperous acres next to the Severances. "A woman and children would be easy pickin's for a bounty hunter like that feller Kirby and his bloodhounds over on Blennerhassett Island. Or Luther Brandon – I hear he's been nosin' around."

"Hell, it could be anyone," pointed out another. "Four hundred and fifty dollars is more than some farmers around here make in a year."

The remaining bleary-eyed abolitionists – farmers, tradesmen, businessmen, professionals, teachers and clergymen – strolled wearily to Severance's spacious barn where their horses were stalled.

"Did you know the land Harness's plantation is on used to be owned by George Washington?" asked the schoolteacher, who had continued to surprise the rest by being one of the long night's survivors.

"Sure, old George was a slaver," remarked the Severances' neighbor. "Jefferson's another. They say black descendants of his live over near Cutler, right here in Washington County."

"Where does it say there in the Declaration of Independence that 'All men are created equal – less'n they're black'?" asked the lumberman, another of the last to leave.

"You have to realize though," argued the teacher, "that times were different then. Many of those Virginia planters treated their slaves quite humanely. There were a number of *free* blacks in that part of the country then too. People forget that the first blacks who came here, back in 1619, came as indentured servants, not as slaves."

"Listen," said Severance, weighing in with one of his rare but pithy pronouncements, "one thing that *don't* change in the human race is greed and inhumanity. That's why there's laws and armies. Slavery's wrong now and it was wrong then, but it's been around since the world began. People will be tryin' to enslave one another, to get somethin' they want and don't have, till hell freezes over."

"Amen," said his neighbor.

"There'll always be people like Harness – north and south alike – and when no one's willing t' stand up to 'em, we're finished," concluded Severance.

"The plague's got us," added Steel.

Snorting, Severance agreed: "That's right – the plague's got us."

15

After our second long night in the wagon we spend most the next day above a tobacco drying shed belong to Rev. Markey a preacher man. I done cut and hang tobacco all my life but I never slept in it before and thats what this like. I dream about being back in Master Harness' fields with that mean old Jeb Porter hanging round when I can sleep which ain't much. I think maybe that strong smell good for Mama's chest though cause she don't cough much all day. Toward evening when Rev. Markey come to get us for supper we hear something just about ruin my appetite. Master Harness and a posse be close by somewhere Rev. Markey say, so instead of spending another night in a wagon we gone be separated round the farm again like at Mr. Palmer's place. We glad we not gone be in that wagon for one night but we sure don't like the idea of Master Harness nosing round. I told you we shouldn't run I tells everybody that done said we should and I can almost feel them riders closing round us. I figure now be more than Alfred and Augustus going down the river, be me and Mama and my whole family. We starts in to arguing amongst ourselves and Alfred speak up like I never heard him before telling us how lucky we is with the underground railroad, folks helping us and giving us this good food and all. To tell the truth I feel a little shamed of myself after that. I eats my dinner without saying much else and later Rev. Markey take Mama my sisters and me to a cave where we done spend the night. Theres blankets and animal skins in there for us so its not too bad but awful damp. Mama done tells us stories when we can't get to sleep and afterwards I sleep like we already safe and sound in Canada.

When Harness crawled from his bedroll the morning after the posse's social call at the Severance farm, Jeb Porter was right there with a cup of steaming coffee. Most of the men were just now getting up, but Harness noticed at once that two or three were missing.

"Where is everybody?"

"Just huntin' us up some meat fer breakfast," replied the overseer.

"Goddamnit, I said no shootin'!"

"You don't think the niggers is somewhere nearby do you?"

"I don't know *where* they are, but we sure as hell won't improve our chances by lettin' 'em know we're here! Which way did they go?"

"Over yonder," said Porter, gesturing vaguely into the woods.

Cursing, Harness threw the rest of his coffee away and yelled to the men still at the campsite: "Fan out and find them hunters! I don't want a single shot fired!"

In the bottom of a draw not far away, a number of giant hardwood trees lay uprooted in a wide swath, toppled by some unimaginable force. From the ridge above, between the fallen trees and the Virginians' campsite, a hunter took aim at a red squirrel high in the boughs of a 300-year-old white oak. Having eaten just bread and bacon the day before, he was determined to make his shot count. He squeezed the trigger of his flintlock, and a few birds exploded from the neighboring trees. The squirrel plummeted into the tangle of fallen timber, not twenty feet from Jane's son Henry, who like his three older brothers had been awakened by the gunshot.

The man who fired it was already sliding down the hillside toward them for breakfast. The brothers held an urgent whispered conference. They couldn't see the hunter to identify him, but he was sure to spot them where they lay on blankets, concealed amongst broken limbs and branches between two massive trunks – and just as likely to hear them if they tried to sneak away.

"I can take 'im!" said Augustus.

"*No* – there may be others with him!" Alfred whispered back.

The family's escape attempt would probably have ended right here were it not for Solomon Harness's dictatorial ways. Alerted to the hunter's location by the gunshot, and enraged by it, he appeared on the ridge in time to see the offender sliding into the tree-strewn ravine after his prey.

"Massa Harness!" exclaimed Henry. Scarcely breathing, he and his three brothers inched themselves back into the cover of the fallen trees as deeply as possible.

"*Did you fire that shot?*" Harness hollered from the ridge.

"...Who – me?" replied the hunter, stopped in the middle of his steep descent. "It weren't me. I *heard* one though."

"Get the hell up here!"

Reluctantly leaving his breakfast behind, the man climbed sheepishly back up the heavily wooded slope as others gathered along the ridge. Harness grabbed hold of the hunter's rifle the moment he reached the top, sniffed the end of its warm barrel and knew at once that it had just been fired.

"You done forfeited your share of the *re*ward," he said, slamming the gun back into the humbled man's hands with a withering look. "If there *is* one, now that we've told the niggers we're here. Let this be a lesson to the rest of you! You're bein' paid for just one thing: to find my slaves and take 'em back with us!"

"You done forfeited your share of the *re*ward," Thornton mimicked him, as Harness and his men turned around on the ridge to head back to camp.

"You done forfeited your chance to *fin' dese* niggahs, Massa Harness," said Augustus. All four of the brothers were giggling maniacally after their close call.

Later that morning when the Virginians rode in from the south, the village of Stafford was quiet – too quiet, Harness suspected. Laid out along Creighton Ridge amidst rolling hills just four years earlier, Stafford had been "Bethel" until the Post Office informed its founders that another community bearing that postmark already existed in Ohio. The present name was resident William Steel's contribution, probably from his Scottish homeland's "Staffordshire."

Stafford was no more than a smattering of clapboard houses at the intersection of Liberty Street and Independence Avenue. Harness eyed each carefully as his posse rode past; he had a strong feeling that his runaway slaves were hiding right here in town. Passing Steel's home, he saw a curtain move downstairs and realized that he and his men were being observed. A band of armed riders was bound to draw attention, but the slaveholder had heard rumors of secret chambers in the Steel house. On impulse he reined his horse around, dismounted and strode up to the door.

Steel was tired and short of patience. He knew that the man knocking peremptorily was Solomon Harness, the reason he'd been up all night at the Severance farm. He took a deep breath before opening the door.

"And what may I do for ye, Sir?" he said upon opening

it, with a forced friendliness he certainly didn't feel.

Somewhat disarmed by the courteous greeting, Harness introduced himself before revealing the reason for his visit. "I'm inquiring if you've seen some niggers wanderin' these parts. Some of my slaves have run off, and I know damn well they're in the area."

"You surely must be mistaken, Sir," replied Steel, affecting amazement. "There are no such people hereabouts, I have never seen such a person as that."

Aware now that he was being mocked, Harness scowled and gestured to his riders. "Then you won't mind if we search your place."

"Not at all, Sir," said Steel – "but first you must attend to a small detail for me."

"And what might that be?" asked Harness suspiciously.

"I'd like you to walk across the street to the funeral parlor and make your final arrangements. For when you search my home and find no 'niggers' here, you'll require its services."

The slaveholder glanced around to see that other men, all of them armed and none of whom appeared the least bit friendly, had materialized between buildings on both sides of the street. Without another word Harness walked back to his horse, swung into the saddle and led his posse out of town, never to return to the peaceful community of Stafford again.

The next day, Harness stopped at a print shop in Marietta to order "Wanted" posters offering a reward of $450 for the return of the fugitives to his Bull Creek plantation: $100 for Alfred, $50 for each of the others.

"I'll send someone over to pick up a hunderd to circulate in Virginia," he said, "and I want another hunderd put up all over Washington County. Can you take care a that?"

"Sure can," said the printer.

"Can you put 'em up where they'll *stay* up?"

"Well now, I can't hardly promise that. I can *try* t' keep 'em away from the abolitionists."

"Tell you what," said Harness. "I'll give you $50 for anyone who catches my niggers on account of this poster."

"You'll give *me* personally $50?" asked the printer incredulously.

"That's what I said."

"You got yerself a deal, Mr. Harness."

The slaveholder didn't answer but turned and walked from the shop. On the long ride back to town the day before, he'd been thinking about what to do next. With the first of his errands accomplished, there was a man he needed to get word to now.

16

As twilight fell on the day of Harness's ignominious retreat from Stafford, Jonas Markey walked into the woods where Jane's sons were hiding and hooted softly like an owl three times. The brothers crept cautiously from the fallen timber.

"Looks like Harness is headin' back to Virginia!" was Jonas' exciting news.

"He *is*?" exclaimed Alfred.

"That's what our scouts say. So we're gonna get you goin' in the other direction."

When Jonas and the brothers arrived back at the barn, they were met not only by their mother and sisters but the Neale couple and their newborn as well. Mrs. Markey introduced them.

"Boys, I'd like you to meet Rose and Howard Neale. They'll be traveling with you for a while – all the way to Canada if mother and baby are up to it."

"Oh we be up to it!" Rose assured her.

The fugitives greeted one another warmly as Mrs. Markey went inside for their evening meal. "We'll have supper for you directly," her husband informed them, "then you have a lot of miles to cover before daylight."

"Mr. an' Mrs. Neale be tellin' us all 'bout how their master done treat his slaves," Jane informed her sons.

"Where y'all from?" asked Thornton.

"Plantation in Washington Bottom downrivah from

Park'sburg," replied Howard Neale. "We taken Marster Neale's name. Done he'ped cross over t' Belpre by a slave woman name of Aunt Jenny. Y'all evah hear tell of Aunt Jenny?"

"*Sho*! we heered of Aunt Jenny!" several of Jane's children volunteered at once.

"Guess ever' slave 'long de rivah knows 'bout Aunt Jenny," said Augustus. "She done blow her horn for y'all?"

"Deed she did," Rose Neale replied. "Marster Stone be waitin' for us soon's we stepped outn de boat. We done hid in his co'nfield till nightfall."

"Dat be three...four nights ago," added her husband. "Just 'bout lost count by now."

"Bet I knows who done row you 'cross!" Henry's grin was infectious. The Neales shared a brief radiant smile, the memory of their own crossing, before turning to be enlightened by the boy.

"Josephus!" he nearly shouted and had to be hushed.

The Neales nodded in agreement. "Dat's de man," said Howard.

"Y'all done run so I guess yo massa not treat you so good," said Alfred, hoping the couple would elaborate.

"...Well, you see, it was like this," said Rose upon securing her husband's mute approval: "we lived in a log cabin with the ground for floors, and the beds be built against the walls like bunks. We slaves had a hard time gettin' food; most times we got just what was left over or whatever Marster Neale wanted to give us, so at night we would slip outn our cabins onto the plantation and kill a pig, a sheep or some cattle that we would butcher in the woods and cut up. Whenever we killed a pig we would have to skin it, because we didn't dare to build a fire. The wimmin folks would carry the eatable pieces back to the cabins in our aprons while the men would stay behind and bury the head and the skin and feet. After gettin' home we would put the meat in special dug trenches and the men would come erelong and cover it up."

"Ain't you feared a haunts out there in de woods at night?" asked Fanny, who was immediately though good-naturedly derided by her brothers.

"Spirits? Well, I believes in 'em all right, but we warant bothered so much by spirits and haunts as we was by wild animals. Why, after it got dark the chillens would have to stay indoors for fear of 'em. The men folks would build a big fire and I can remember my pappy a sittin' on top of the house with a old flintlock 'cross his legs awaitin' for one of them critters to come close enough sos he could shoot it. He was trusted with a gun because he was raised by the poor white man who worked for Marster Neale. My pappy drove a team of horses, he didn't work in the fields."

The fugitives talked on until Jonas and Mrs. Markey brought their food, and when the generous meal was over, Jane, her daughters, Rose Neale and the baby all squeezed together in the bottom of the wagon. Jonas was to drive the next leg of their journey.

"Thankee kindly," said Jane, her eyes glistening – "weuns'll nevah foget what you done fo us."

"We only did what was right, Jane," replied Mrs. Markey.

"We'll pray for you and your family," her husband promised them – "and for you young folks too."

"Thank the Lord your little one will never know the burden of slavery," added his wife.

"We thank the Lord, and we thank the Underground Railroad, Mizz Markey," said Howard Neale.

"God bless all of you," she said, twisting her apron in slender weathered hands.

Jonas nodded to Alfred and Augustus, and the brothers pulled the stiff, acrid-smelling canvas over the women. Then he shook the reins, and the big draft horses pulled together to begin another long night on the road.

Alfred, armed with a pitchfork, and Augustus and Howard, carrying clubs, strode along in front of the team of horses. The moon was nearly full, bathing the landscape in more light than conductors preferred for night travel. But spies had confirmed that Harness's men had taken the ferry back to Virginia late that afternoon, and it had been decided that the greater risk would be for the passengers – including the Neales, brought over from the Severance farm earlier in the day – to tarry any longer than absolutely necessary.

Now, somewhere below the ridge road to the Summerfield Station, the fugitives' next destination, whippoorwills called mournfully to one another. In the distance a fox yelped, while pressing upon the travelers from all sides, a nocturnal chorus of katydids, crickets and, where there was water, tree frogs thrummed in the night. Suddenly the horses stopped in their tracks. Snorting, jerking their heads, they strained against the reins, threatening to bolt.

Jonas, holding the horses momentarily with one hand, pulled a small single-shot pistol from his pocket with the other and placed it within easy reach on the footrest. Everyone peered into the darkness to see what had spooked the horses.

"What you think it is?" asked Alfred.

Struggling to control the big draft horses, Jonas didn't answer at first, then cried out: "There it is!"

A large dog or wolf staggered unsteadily toward them on the moonlit road. Less than 50 yards ahead, it stopped to utter a blood-curdling sound, more gurgle than growl. The animal was in extreme pain or misery – obviously rabid.

"*Mad dog*!" exclaimed Augustus.

"May be a wolf!" said Thornton in an awed, fearful whisper.

In 1843, some 40 years before Pasteur's discovery of a

vaccine against rabies, a rabid dog was one of the most dangerous animals in the world. Likely to attack at any moment, its bite was invariably lethal, one reason nearly every wagon on the road carried a pitchfork.

"Whatever it is, it be rabid all right. Git in de wagon, you two!" Alfred ordered Henry and Thornton, who needed no coaxing.

"Why we stoppin'?" asked Jane in a muffled voice from the wagon.

"Mad dog, Mama!" replied Henry as he and Thornton scrambled aboard.

"*Mad dog*?" Jane struggled to sit up beneath the heavy canvas.

"It's all right, Mama!" yelled Alfred. "Y'all stay in de wagon!"

Having encountered rabid animals before, Alfred was thankful for the pitchfork in his hands and for the moonlight. "Look like he fixin' t' charge, Gus – lemme take 'im on first! Then you know what t' do wid dat club."

"I be ready," said Augustus, hefting the heavy hickory branch.

When the dog finally sprang, Alfred met it squarely with the tines of the pitchfork, driving them deep into the suffering beast's neck and chest. He didn't have to say another word to Augustus. Once the drooling, snarling animal was immobilized his younger brother rushed in to beat it savagely in the head until its contorted, writhing body lay still at last.

"Dat's enough, 'Gustus – he dead now," said Alfred, breathing heavily. "It's all right now, Mama! 'Gustus done kilt it!" he called to his mother.

The two younger boys jumped from the wagon and stood over the dead animal transfixed.

"What happen if'n he done bite one a we?" asked Henry.

"Den you go mad, jus' lak him," replied Augustus.

"We have to kill Henry?" asked Thornton. His younger brother couldn't tell which disturbed him more: the question or the morbid fascination in Thornton's tone of voice.

"Best fo Henry if'n we do kill 'im, if he be mad," said Alfred. Henry took all this in and shuddered.

Jonas regained control of the trembling horses, and the fugitives set off again into the night. A few hours later the wagon reached the station at Summerfield, where Richard, Thomas and William Horton, William Capell, and John Lemmax were principal stationmasters on the Underground Railroad. All had brought their families to Noble County from Ireland.

Also among the early population of this area were a number of pro-slavery descendants of families from Virginia. Since in their bitter opposition to abolition they were sure to help return fugitive slaves to their legal owners, stationmasters had to be especially careful in this part of the county. A dug-out cellar beneath the smaller of William Horton's two barns was often used to hide runaway slaves in Summerfield.

"Dis damp cellar be bad fo yo cough, Mama," said Rachel, fixing a bed for Jane, whose congestion had worsened during the night.

"We on'y be heah fo de day," said Jane with a gesture of dismissal. "Den where Massa Horton say we headed?"

"To Guinea, Mizz Jane," Rose Neale replied. "Mistah Horton say no bounty hunters come *near* Guinea."

An all-black community in Belmont County some 15 miles to the northeast, Guinea was really the first station where fugitives were able to relax; officials of the freedom line considered it a haven where bounty hunters dared not venture.

While waiting for their meal, Caroline enviously

watched Rose lift her newborn to cradle the hungry infant against her breast. "...Ah'm gwine have a baby," she said shyly to the young mother when Rose, feeling her ardent gaze, looked up from her suckling child.

"You is? Well, good fo you, girl!"

"Mah man an' me, we 'bout t' jump de broom. But he have t' stay behin', care fo his mothah."

"You make it okay – you gots yo fam'ly with you."

"What yo baby's name?"

"Don' know yet," replied Rose, sharing a smile with her husband – "still tryin' t' think of de right one."

"...What's it *like* – feedin' an' all?"

"Oh, it's not lak I thought it be. Ah *nevah* felt sumpin' lak dis befo....Ah'm glad she not grow up t' be no slave."

Caroline glanced over to see whether her mother had overheard. Jane's expression was not "I told you so" but a rare glimpse of unguarded love for her eldest daughter – as well as an exhausted determination that she, too, would bestow this gift upon her family.

17

We meets the nicest folks name of Rose and Howard Neale when Rev. Markey roust us out the cave we spend the night and most the next day in waiting on Master Harness and his posse to leave. The worst part is knowing they close by but not knowing where. One day in that cave seem almost like a whole week on the plantation. But Rev. Markey come get us at last and thats when we meet the Neales with their little baby that still don't have a name. I watch Rose nurse her little girl and I get a funny feeling like its me and my own. She tell me it be like nothing else she know and I can surely believe that. Seeing how tender her husband be with Rose and her baby make me start missing my man again but I know my life changing a little every day we gets closer to Canada where my own baby be born. Thats what I think most about now not how life be back on the plantation.

Thats where Master Harness headed glory be, back to Virginia with his hired riders, but there still be bounty hunters we needs to hide from Rev. Markey say, so down under the canvas we goes again on what be our third night on the road. I asleep when I hear Mama scream mad dog and I come up out of there so fast that stiff canvas rub my nose raw but Alfred and Augustus kill it before it bites anyone. Mama's cough done came back in that cave at Rev. Markey's and it gets worse where they put us next, an old damp cellar at the Horton farm in a place called Summerfield. We all starting to worry about her cause Mama hardly ever be sick before and never for longer than a day or two but she been feeling poorly since we done crossed the river.

Late the morning of the fugitives' arrival in Summerfield, a hulking pro-slavery opportunist named Luther Brandon was talking to the proprietor of a general store in Carlisle, a village a few miles to the southwest.

"There's a substantial *re*ward, Brandon, that's all I can tell you," said the intense-looking little man. "They crossed the river four days ago, so if they're headin' to Canada they could be around here somewheres. I'd try over to the Hortons' if I was you. You *know* the Hortons is nigger lovers."

"I just might do that, Amos. And if you're right, there might be a piece a that *re*ward money in it for you." Brandon winked at a man waiting behind him at the counter as he lumbered to the door.

"Uh huh. Tecumseh mighta been a Quaker too," said the proprietor without emotion.

Brandon guffawed. "Shoot, Amos, you ain't a castin' doubt on my good intentions are ya?" he tossed back over his shoulder.

"Good intentions and good credit," said the proprietor to his other customer: "two things Luther Brandon wouldn't know from the hind-end of a copperhead."

Having decided to put the Summerfield Station under surveillance, Brandon rode to within half a mile of the Horton farm, where he tied his horse to a tree with sufficient slack in the reins for it to graze. Then he hiked through the woods to a knoll overlooking the farmhouse, barns and outbuildings. Sitting down on the ground, he took out his pocketknife and began to whittle, while keeping an eye on the buildings below.

Almost two hours later the crude but recognizable head of a wolf had emerged from the small basswood branch Brandon was working on, and his patience hadn't even been tested yet. Nor would it be: when he looked up from his handiwork, he spotted Rose Neale, holding her baby, emerge from the cellar to relieve herself in an outhouse nearby.

Standing up in excitement, the bounty hunter murmured to himself: "Damned if I don't have half a mind to give you a taste of that *re*ward after all, Amos!"

Although he'd guessed right, Brandon knew that he couldn't capture the slaves by himself – he'd already lost a fight to the biggest Horton brother, Thomas – and as it was late afternoon by now, he didn't have time to go for reinforcements. His best alternative was to wait until nightfall to see which way the runaways were headed, then ride for help to one of the pro-slavery farms in the area and try to head the wagon off before it reached its destination in the morning.

A little later Brandon learned how the fugitives had arrived when a team of horses, with Jonas Markey at the reins, pulled an empty wagon from one of the outbuildings and clattered away. As the afternoon wore on and he continued to watch the farm from his hiding place, Brandon observed several members of Jane's family answer nature's call. Eventually, their evening meal was brought to them in a large picnic basket. The rumors had been right: there were a number of slaves in the cellar; a large reward would be his to share if they could be captured.

What Brandon hadn't counted on was that on his return to Summerfield with the wagon Jonas would spot the bounty hunter's horse tethered well off the road in the woods. Had the sound of the wagon not prompted the animal to whinny, Jonas would probably never have seen it. As it was, when he got down to investigate and recognized the big Morgan stallion as Brandon's from the initials L.B. on the saddle, Jonas realized at once why it was here. He removed the saddle and bridle and turned the horse loose. It immediately cantered off toward Carlisle and home.

While Luther Brandon limped back to Carlisle, shifting the weight of his saddle and bridle from one aching shoulder to the other, most of Jane's pain arose from within. The demands of motherhood and the journey couldn't entirely prevent her from brooding deeply over the bleak, often cruel memories which the constant work and fatigue of slavery had usually kept at bay. But there was another deterrent to depression that was more effective: the faint glimmer of a feeling utterly new and foreign to her. It had taken Jane some time over the past few days to identify this mood or intuition or sensation even when it finally breached the threshold of perception, like the imperceptibly rising waters of a flood. But at some point her mind finally acknowledged what her heart had been telling her for days: this was *freedom* she was feeling, for the first time in her life.

Not only was she seeing an unfamiliar landscape, new people and places for the first time in more than 30 years, but in a sense that had never really been true before, the images Jane's eyes hungrily lingered on were *hers*, they belonged to her. The very air she breathed, the wind in her face were hers to savor as she pleased. And she and her family could go – they were *free* to go – wherever the wind took them. The thought of this was both exhilarating and unnerving, even terrifying when she followed it too far. For where there were no more chains, there was also no longer the corrupt and meager security that life on the Harness plantation had held for her family. In place of walls, endless labor, a life of unbreakable rules and routine, there was....The mutable image that had sometimes come to Jane in trying to imagine freedom and the future was bound up with her picture of Canada: a frozen wasteland like the Ohio River iced over in winter. It had visited her in dreams as a horizonless, treeless plain which then turned into an empty plate, empty plates on an empty table. Then Jane had to draw herself up, make herself strong, remind herself that Canada was a land freer even than Ohio, where no bounty hunters would be able to grab her children and drag them back into slavery.

May 30, 1864

My Dear Brother Thornton,

Been doing a lot of thinking lately, on foot in our endless dust-stifling strung-out columns and at night for hours instead of sleeping, exhausted though I am – of how Mama must have felt when she gathered up her great courage and led us all to freedom. These and many other thoughts come teeming through my brain as if I have the fever. My mind is like a battlefield in its own way these days, full of a disorder approaching chaos, yet somehow peaceful at the same time if you can understand that. I guess maybe it's because I have surrendered on my personal battlefield to chaos as natural in my situation. What situation is that, you may ask. And I reply: the brink of some great change in my life, Thorn, a transition I can sense as readily as if it were by one of the five senses we acknowledge, though it must surely be another, intuition perhaps, which I now believe to be as real as the others.

How could we children not have realized the kind of quandary Mama faced before crossing that river? The damned if she do, damned if she don't kind of decision she had to make with the lives of every one of her children in the balance. Were the older ones aware of this? Were you? Was I the only one who although with some notion of Mama's courage in running off with us, failed to realize that even getting safely to Canada wouldn't end her worries but be the beginning of a whole new kind? Here was a woman raised her whole life in slavery, with the mouths of we three youngest to feed at least, who was going to have to learn a whole new way to live. How could I have been so ignorant, even as just a kid, of how scary the idea of freedom could be to one completely unaccustomed to it, when I had observed how the birds and critters we used to catch and keep in cages for awhile would often hesitate to leave them when it came time to let them go? As scared at first to trade cage for freedom again as they'd been of their captors in the first place. And Mama had known nothing <u>but</u> the cage for more than 50 years! Now after all that time she was pushing her own self out of the nest so to speak. Trusting wings she had never tried to hold her up. So I'm still getting to know her, Thornton, after all these years. Is that true of you too?

As for myself, I'm like a twig in a river – not complaining, you understand. This is what I wanted when I enlisted, and for a long time it didn't look like I was ever going to become a real soldier allowed to fight for what I believe in. I will say it's certainly not like I imagined it, but then nothing of any complexity is ever the way it appears (Oberlin was a revelation). I was prepared for disparity between my conception of fighting and the reality of warfare. But not the magnitude, Thorn. I was prepared for death (or thought I was) and dying, even to some extent for having to kill. But there was no way to have prepared myself for the utter waste of life I have experienced these past few weeks. Men come to terms with this, if at all, either by denying the possibility of succumbing to it, of falling in battle; or as I have, by what I spoke of at the beginning of this letter. By surrendering to a new perception of life, which at first seemed so ghastly and terrible but has since become, as I've accepted it, a new world seen through new eyes. In such chaos there's no way to know anything as fixed as "answers" and no real desperation behind one's questions. Am I to live, or die? What lies beyond this life, the only one I've known? Where will the river I'm caught up in take this humble twig? I know only that I love you, Thorn, and that I finally have some sense now of what our mother went through to make us all free. My love and admiration for her continue to grow as I still grow.

Your loving brother,
Henry

Beginning the second week of the escape: Saturday-Tuesday night

18

Jane's family and the Neales pulled into Guinea just before daybreak and were soon comfortably seated around a large table laden with steaming cups of sassafras tea and plates heaped with hot cornpone. With a black population large enough to protect itself from invasion by slave hunters, Guinea was the first station on the Washington-Monroe-Belmont County branch of the Underground Railroad where the fugitives could relax somewhat and talk freely. Until now, their every activity had been concerned with either hiding or the stealth of night travel, with minimal whispered conversation.

"Ain't much of a breakfast," said their host, Ma Harper, a light-skinned mulatto, "but I promise you-uns a fittin' supper." Molly Harper, who acquired her nickname helping innumerable fugitive slaves pass through the Guinea Underground Railroad station, had never been a slave herself, having been born free in Southampton County, Virginia, in 1790. Her late husband Jacob, who died in 1838 at the age of 52, had also been free, by manumission. But the truth was, they had been too close to events surrounding the Nat Turner rebellion 12 years earlier. The Harpers and 20 free relatives had left Virginia the day before the bloody uprising began, fearing that something would go wrong and innocent people, both black and white, would suffer. In Brunswick County they had met an abolitionist on his way to Wheeling in western

Virginia. He offered to escort the party to the Ohio River, passing them off as his slaves to make the journey less complicated. Crossing the Ohio into Belmont County, the free Negroes found work as farmers around the Quaker settlement of Barnesville before establishing the small black community of Guinea a few miles to the south.

Ma Harper was tall for a woman of the time and had retained her youthful figure. She could read and write and retained some knowledge of her Ethiopian heritage. She told her visitors how her great, great-grandfather had been tricked into coming to Virginia in the 1650s. When he arrived in the New World, attempts had been made to enslave him, but he'd outsmarted his adversaries to achieve the status of indentured servant and after 10 years was freed. He'd even owned a modest tobacco plantation and for a few generations his descendants had prospered. Eventually, however, jealous European immigrants had stolen the family's land and unsuccessfully tried to impose slavery on Molly's ancestors. Her father had worked as a sharecropper most of his life. She married Jacob Harper, a carpenter by trade, at age 18 and the young couple had settled into raising a family.

Jacob's white father Robert, the owner of Carter's Grove Plantation in Southampton County, traced his ancestry back to William the Conqueror. Freed at the age of 10, Jacob had stayed on the plantation and was paid a small wage along with his board. When he left home at the age of 14, he vowed to return and buy his mother's freedom. She declined his offer, which she knew to be sincere, advising the boy to learn a trade such as carpentry, blacksmithing or stonemasonry, as both slaves and free Negroes were given the opportunity to do in Virginia at the time. Although a few years later Robert Carter freed all 500 of his slaves – the largest recorded manumission until the Civil War – Jacob's mother remained on his plantation, serving her former owner for the rest of her life.

Jacob was well-acquainted with Nat Turner, a preacher who commanded great respect among the slaves and free blacks around Southampton County. Molly's husband might very well have been drawn into the four-day insurrection with the rest of Turner's 70 or so followers but for her insistence that it was bound for certain failure. The solar eclipse which Turner believed to be his call to action as the servant of a vengeful god was not, for Molly, a sign that he would achieve anything but violence and destruction. The Harpers, who hated the institution of slavery, not white people themselves, were deeply saddened, as much by the slaughter of more than 50 whites as by the considerably larger number of innocent blacks killed in retaliation.

Ma Harper was brought sharply back to 1843 when Jane commented on the wooden floor of her cabin. "Yes," replied Ma, "my late husband took the time to build that. He was a fine carpenter in his day. He's the one taught me to read and write and do some figures too."

Jane's children's eyes lighted up with such talk. "I learnt some!" exclaimed Alfred.

"Learnt some what?" chided Jane. "What good that readin' and writin' gonna do you iffen you don't have no manners."

"No, no, it's good to learn," insisted Ma. "We folks cain't learn too much. We need to know sech things as what's goin' on with the Abolitionist movement." She handed Alfred a copy of the latest *Liberator*, the Abolitionist journal published by William Lloyd Garrison, in which the great black orator Frederick Douglass often wrote anti-slavery articles.

"Dang!" exclaimed Alfred, "dis here sho nuff hard to read." He stammered from word to word with Ma correcting and encouraging him as he read the short article

"Free Men of Color Fight Slavery" aloud to his family.

One of the best-provided stations on the Underground Railroad, Guinea was offering the runaways their first taste of real freedom. Most stations were forced to hide their passengers in cold dark cellars or caves or drafty barns for extended periods while bounty hunters lurked about, but Jane's family and the Neales were each given the use of a comfortable cabin. Due to the late summer season, there was no shortage or lack of variety of food, and the nearby Quaker community around Barnesville provided the runaways with clothing and other essential items.

From Guinea the fugitives fled northward the next day to the Judge Robert Collins farm west of Barnesville, an Ohio community founded by Quakers in 1800. It rained most of the night, and the two big draft horses, pulling yet another in the succession of wagons that had served Jane's family like detached coaches on a night train to Canada, had to struggle at times for footing. The narrow road's deep ruts had liquefied to a thick soup of clay that sucked at their hooves and the wheels of the canvas-covered wagon. At the foot of Mt. Ephriam, the last big hill they would encounter on their journey, Jane and her daughters were finally compelled to get out and climb beside the wagon. Even Aaron, their conductor, had to drive the horses up the steep winding grade from the ground. Trees and underbrush crowding the roadside continually forced the travelers back into muck which in some places was halfway to the knees of the smaller children. Alfred and Augustus had to lift them from under their armpits to pull them out.

An Underground Railroad crossroads where runaway slaves from the south and east were gathered before being sent northward to Oberlin, Barnesville had been involved in the abolitionist movement from the town's beginning. Quakers had often purchased young slaves at the Wheeling auction, taught them to read and write, then given them their freedom papers – as had Collins himself, a U.S. Circuit Court judge who conducted two weeks of court proceedings every three months in Columbus.

After spending the day in the hayloft of Judge Collins's barn, the fugitives traveled all night to Freeport, in Harrison County. Hidden in a small barn close to the woods, they could see field hands harvesting sorghum and smell its sweet juice from the boiling-sheds all day long.

The following night's uneventful journey ended just before dawn near the German village of Gnadenhutten in Tuscarawas County. In the afternoon free blacks homesteading on a neighboring farm stopped by to chat. They wanted to know what life had been like for the fugitives as slaves. Did their master beat them or treat them kindly? How much freedom were they given? Did they get Sundays off for church and to tend their gardens or were they even allowed a garden of their own? And how had the Neales kept their baby from giving them all away?

"Laudanum," replied Howard; "but we only had to give it to her once so far."

"She been a li'l angel," declared her mother, gently rocking the smiling, still unnamed infant.

Jane's children had just as many questions for their interrogators. What was it like in Canada, was it really as cold as everybody said? What kind of clothes would they need to stay warm? Would they have a place to stay? This free exchange was as valuable as the information itself; they were in a different world now. A new life.

"Will there be any more bounty hunters after us?" Thornton wanted to know. And Henry, feeling safe enough now for bluster, chided him for being such a scare baby. "Alfred and 'Gustus take care of anyone try to stop us now," he boasted for the benefit of their appreciative audience. "They put 'em beneath the ground befo' lettin' anyone keep us from gettin' safe to Canady."

"Oh, don't say that, youngun!" one of the free blacks admonished him. "You be safe in Canada if all you is is a slave done run away. But if'n you commits a crime they can taken you back."

"Say nothin' of killin' a white man," added another.

"You should be safe enough now you gotten this far," someone else chimed in. "The fuhther north you gets the safer you be. Just be mindin' what yo conductors tells you an' do lak they say. You be seein' that 'ere blue water sho enough."

The clandestine get-together left the Neales and Jane's family stirred up and restless with anticipation. Afterwards Alfred fidgeted and paced for awhile in the loft where they were hiding out, then sat off by himself with a tormented expression that was most unlike his normal disposition. One after another of his brothers and sisters were rebuffed when they tried to learn what was troubling him. Jane and most of Alfred's siblings had fallen asleep when Augustus finally sat down beside him in the loose straw. Although Augustus neither addressed nor even looked at him, Alfred could feel his empathy as clearly as if the weight of his brother's muscular arm lay across his shoulders.

"...Been thinkin' on our daddy," Alfred said at last. "Funny, but I hain't thought a dat man...don't know how long it's been."

"Dat right?" said Augustus.

A long pause ensued before Alfred suddenly spoke out again in a voice tight with emotion. "I feel shamed of myself, 'Gustus. Somehow all dese years I been holdin' it ag'in our daddy dat he let hisself get sent down rivah an' leave us all behin'. Like dat make him less of a man. Like it be shameful on *his* part."

Augustus said nothing though his eyes widened perceptibly at Alfred's confession.

"I thought the world of dat man," continued his brother. "But somehow I done clean fo'got about all de good things. Just put de man out'n mah mind – like he done nevah even live almos'."

Augustus gazed straight ahead into dust-laden shafts of afternoon sunlight slanting through the gloom of the barn, afraid or unwilling to turn his head. Because of the high-pitched quality, the near sob in Alfred's tone of voice, which threatened to unman Augustus as well. He had no memory of their father but he knew exactly what his brother was talking about, though they had never discussed this between themselves, as children, as boys or as young men. Why had it come out now, so unexpectedly?

"How could a man do dat, 'Gustus? Put his own daddy out of mind like he nevah even alive?...Course Mama nevah done talk about him. You an' me, an' Rachel an' Caroline nevah talk about him....Ah used t' ride around on Pappy's shoulders fo you even bo'n. De worl' sho look good from up dere, I didn't know nothin' 'bout slavery. I just know Pappy de biggest, strongest man on de place – and Mama de softest. Not lak now. Not lak she been since seem like fo'evah. Back den, two of 'em lak a roof ovah mah head....Den t' see Pappy go up into dat boat ...his back just a bleedin' and all cut up...Mama standin' dere, sayin' nothin', maybe a tear but not a sound out of her...I didn't know what t' think. 'Cept Pappy musta done somethin' wrong an' got whupped for it an' sent away. And I just...after dat I just put him outa mah mind, 'Gustus – like I thought Mama done too, 'cause she nevah talk about him. Nevah say a word 'bout him."

Augustus knew he should tell his brother that he wasn't alone, that whatever had happened to drive their father from his mind as surely as Master Harness had driven him from their lives, it had happened to all of them, not just to Alfred alone. But he couldn't speak of this himself at the moment, didn't even want to try – besides, he could sense his brother mastering his feelings now. No more was said between them that day. But although they avoided each other, Alfred had in fact heard Augustus and been comforted by his articulate, uncontesting silence.

Even though we no longer so afraid of being caught this running be hard on all of us. The fifth day I believe it was we taken in at a place called Guinea where black folks lives free and proud, just as natural as the day is long. Guinea be a special place for all of us, I guess we never really believe it till we see it for ourselves, nothing but black folks living and working making a life for theyselves the way they wants, no white master or overseer standing over them telling them this the way it got to be, you mine. You all can do the same thing in Canada they say, freedom the best thing in the world. Thornton say why can't we stay here stead of going all the way to Canada? Cause you don't have no freedom papers they tell him, you might get caught and taken back, some white folks bothers us enough as it is when we away from here. But no one gone take us someone else say and we all see they mean it.

Next night it rain so hard we all gets wet, cover don't do no good. Then we has to get out the wagon and walk up some damn steep hill in the rain. Next day Mama not the only one coughing and blowing their nose. We dry off in a hayloft belong to a judge name of Collins. Never knew hay could feel so good. We in a barn the next day too, Fanny and Henry be wild from the smell of sweet sorghum somewhere but it make me near sick to death, Mama say it from the baby. Days start to get all mixed up in my mind, one just like the next, we sure tired of running and hiding.

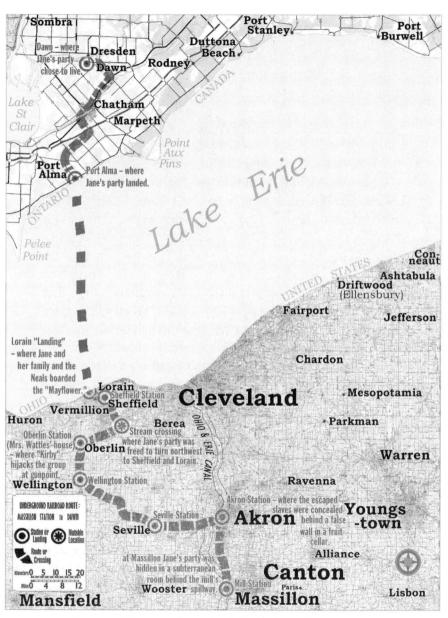

The end of the second, and beginning of the third, week of
the escape: Wednesday-Monday night

19

Too easy. Though she didn't express her concern in these or any words even to herself, this was the gist of the uneasiness Jane was feeling in her bones. After the triumph of landing safely on Ohio soil and finding her family embraced by people as competent and fearless as they were caring in their obvious desire to help the fugitives escape...after the indescribable relief accompanying this initial success, some small voice, some instinct at the core of perception whispered to her that it had all come too easily.

Of course the entirety of her experience prevented Jane from relaxing for a moment. And this nagging sense of doubt was becoming more pronounced with each new dawn, with almost every mile, it seemed, that her family put between themselves and the life they were fleeing. As if some essential element of their lives unalterably connected to slavery, something Jane had overlooked or was unconscious of, were being stretched to the breaking point. When this centuries-old umbilical cord finally parted would the result be catastrophic in some way for her family? Some way she kept trying to imagine so as to be prepared for it, to prevent the worst from happening? How could she have waited so long to run, how could slavery survive and sustain itself, if it were really this easy to escape?

Nevertheless, despite Jane's profound misgivings, the runaways traveled that night, on foot and in a wagon with a false bottom beneath a load of hay, from Gnadenhutten to Dover, where they were put up over a store right in the middle of town. None of the younger children could sleep the next day; they all sat at windows watching the unfamiliar goings-on of a busy northern town from behind thin muslin curtains.

The following night the fugitives traveled for a while along the towpath beside the Ohio and Erie Canal. When on two occasions they encountered barges tied up for the night, the men melted into the woods and gave them a wide berth. Near daybreak they arrived at a feed and grain mill near Massillon, in Stark County. While the miller helped the women from the wagon, one of his sons diverted water from the millrace just above the massive waterwheel which was the motive power of the mill's intricate system of cogwheels and gears. Bypassing the wheel, the water now ran freely through a shallow ditch that channeled it back into the stream about thirty feet away. And beneath the wheel, where a curtain of falling water had concealed it, was the entrance to a large subterranean room, secure but with walls wet to the touch.

"Wear dis, Mama," said Alfred, draping his long-sleeved linsey-woolsey shirt around Jane's shoulders. "Feels like it be fixin' t' rain in here."

When the fugitives were safely inside the hidden chamber, the stream was released over the millwheel again. The creaking and groaning of its water-borne revolutions threatened to drive the weary travelers slowly mad during the day. But their spirits were lifted by a hearty breakfast. And after the miller's wife gave them plenty of clean, dry feed sacks to lie on to ward off the dampness and chill, the day of seclusion turned out to be one of the most restful of their trip so far. The reverberations of the waterwheel following the full meal soon lulled every one of the fugitives to sleep.

That night Jane's family and the Neales were taken by a free black conductor named Charles Grant to a farmhouse on the outskirts of Akron, where they were put up for the day in the concealed half of a double basement. The large dirt-walled room was sealed off by planks from a fruit cellar which neighbors, some of them pro-slavery, had visited many times. The next night saw a change in direction: due west, to Seville, instead of the northerly heading the runaways had been following since crossing the Ohio River ten nights earlier.

The past week or so, with one day and night flowing into the next in a maze of dusty roads and musty hiding places had been marked more by tedium and fatigue than tension or fear. The round of grueling nights followed by days spent in fitful slumber had all begun to seem alike to Jane and her family: kind people; usually good and plentiful food; hideouts ranging from secret chambers with clean comfortable bedding on the floor to cold dank cellars. Jane's cough had become progressively worse, often accompanied now by a fever and shivering fits.

Even this far north there was good reason, she learned, for her continuing apprehension. In nearby Wooster, pro-slavery neighbors of an Underground Railroad station-master named Robert Taggart had burned his barn to the ground in protest. Spies and slave hunters regularly compelled conductors to alter their routes. On the other hand, she was told, James Rose, an Ashland County man tired of feeling like a thief in conducting runaway slaves to and from his home, often carried fugitives openly in his wagon in broad daylight, despite the taunts and threats of some of his neighbors. Because of the large reward posted for them, however, such brazen behavior was clearly out of the question in connection with Jane's family. It was once again by night, and in secret, that they were taken northwest from Seville to Wellington just ten miles from

Oberlin, a short night's journey from Lake Erie.

No mere accident of geography had made the small college town of Oberlin a principal northern terminus of the Underground Railroad. Ever since its founding ten years earlier Oberlin Collegiate Institute, as the school was called at first, had been known for its fundamental religious and antislavery position. And with more than a thousand students (most of them the sons and daughters of Ohio farmers) and their professors comprising a large segment of its population, the town itself had the same reputation. Unlike most towns its size, Oberlin had no saloons, and the principal hotel was owned by the college, which forbade the sale not only of alcoholic beverages but of tobacco as well. In fact smoking in public was illegal within the city limits.

Although, with its neat white houses surrounded by gardens and picket fences, the town resembled the New England villages many of its residents had come from, what set it apart were Oberlin's many black students and townspeople. The community was Ohio's most fully integrated, with black voters, black and white children attending the same public schools; black and white parishioners praying and sitting together in First Church; and the gravestones of black men and women intermingled with those of deceased white residents in Westwood Cemetery.

All this had been explained to the Neales and Jane's family by the time they arrived at the home of Esther Wattles, a widow with three daughters who had helped many runaway slaves to freedom. Though the town was not as safe for them as the all-black community of Guinea had been, after nearly two weeks of flight from slavery, with Lake Erie and freedom so close, Oberlin seemed a sanctuary to Jane nonetheless. She began to breathe easier in spite of herself as her children were led upstairs to the large airy room they would share until nightfall.

But, ironically, it was Oberlin's reputation and strategic location on the Underground Railroad that were about to make Jane's family more vulnerable than at any time since crossing the Ohio River. After losing their trail in southeast Ohio, Solomon Harness had decided that Oberlin represented his last and best chance to apprehend his escaped slaves. There was, after all, a virtually unlimited combination of northerly routes across Ohio that the fugitives could have taken, but less than half a dozen towns upon which these lines all converged at the end of the journey. And the most likely destination, of course, was the town considered the safest.

So it was to Oberlin that Harness had dispatched the notorious bounty hunter from Blennerhassett Island known only by the last name of Kirby. Having set off a week before with enough of Harness's money to hire help if necessary in recapturing the runaways, Kirby had been in town now for two days. To most residents the swarthy, sinister-looking stranger had come to Oberlin to buy timber from various farms in the area. But there were pro-slavery people in the outlying countryside – the same who a year ago had tried to have Oberlin College's charter revoked – who had been watching the roads for him.

20

The sense of excitement inside the modest clapboard house had risen to such intensity that Rachel imagined the roof beginning to vibrate and rattle like the lid on a kettle. Her older sister's thoughts were drawn to their destination, the new home she herself would provide some day. Caroline held her hands to her abdomen and tried to picture her baby-to-be. Like the ship they were about to board, like the endless wagon train that had carried them northward across Ohio, she bore a precious cargo.

Esther and her daughters were accustomed to the anticipation of runaway slaves about to embark on the voyage of liberation for which they had risked everything, but never before a family as large as Jane's. The Wattleses had fallen in love with them at once, spending the day feeding them, distributing warm clothing collected in the community, preparing them not only for the final leg of their long dangerous journey but for their new home in Canada as well.

As usual, Henry and Thornton asked the most questions of their hosts. Fanny said little though her eyes seemed to grow larger with each new piece of information about the transformation about to take place in their lives. Christian miracle, witch doctor's magic, West African fable: their trip across the water and the new world it would open up to her held a little of all of these. She couldn't quite believe that it would all come to pass.

"Dis here boat come jus' for weuns?" Henry asked Alice, one of the Wattles sisters, who was helping him into a patched wool jacket that fit tolerably well with the sleeves rolled up.

"No, bless your heart," she replied. "It will be carrying paying passengers and cargo too. Those lake steamers can't afford to cross with nothing but slaves aboard. They'd go out of business."

"Glad dis won't be just another skiff like de las' time," said Thornton. "River wanted in dat boat sumpin fierce. We had t' bail water de whole time."

"Ain't nevah been on no steamship befo'!"

"You'll be on a steamship all right," the young woman assured Henry, "but where you'll board we won't know till tonight."

"What you mean, Missus?" asked Augustus, who like his siblings had been following the conversation attentively.

"Well you see, we often don't know till just a few hours before you leave which steamship you'll be on – and that determines what port you'll be taken to. The closest is Lorain, just 12 miles north by the most direct route. But it's safer through Sheffield to the east of here, because that way *isn't* direct."

"Where else they may taken us, Missus?" asked Augustus.

"Huron is the farthest west you'd go," said Alice, "by way of Florence to Lyman Scott's station. He can put you aboard a steamship on the Huron River; it runs into the lake there. No one would see you because there are heavy woods between Mr. Scott's barn and the river."

"Another place is Vermillion, between Huron and Lorain," offered Mabel, the oldest sister, who had just entered the room with their supper. "They built a pier for steamships at the mouth of the Vermillion River two years ago."

"Then of course to the east you have Cleveland,"

continued Alice. "There's even a lighthouse there now. Must be more than 10,000 people in Cleveland – too crowded for me."

The late summer day was frustratingly slow in taking its leave. Jane had come to notice, when she was able to glimpse one, that sunsets tended to linger the farther north they traveled. How long ago it had been – surely more than two weeks, it seemed more like two months – since she'd mustered all her courage to break the news to her children. It was about this time of day when she'd left the tobacco field for the last time, then gone up to the big house to see what Mrs. Harness might need. The last time she would do that gracious but demanding lady's bidding without question or complaint. On that day, too, a body of water had lain before them, both obstacle and portal to a promised land. A body of water between her family and freedom.

As she thought ahead to what was supposed to happen tonight and tried to assess what might possibly go wrong, Jane was aware of a feeling in her heart that was at once peaceful yet fierce in some way too, mysterious though familiar. She felt surer now than at any time before or during their run to freedom that they would reach Canada safely. Yet there was a sense of danger in her premonition as well. Not the constant fearful state of alert that had permeated her every waking moment since she'd gathered up her family and fled into the night; something nearer, sharper. And, strangely, one was part of the other: the thrill of danger made her intuition more believable, helped her trust it. While her faith in a safe arrival held her fear in check.

It was about 8:30, not yet quite dark, when the sound of a wagon abruptly ended all conversation.

"That can't be Robins Burrell already, can it?" Esther Wattles exclaimed. "It's not even dark yet."

"It must be Mr. Burrell, Mama. We'd best hurry and get these folks ready," said her eldest daughter, gesturing for the Neales and Jane's family to get their things together.

"See who it is, Eliza," her mother told the youngest of the three girls.

The 12-year-old, her cheeks flushed with excitement, opened the door quickly and ran out to greet the wagon just as it drew up before the house. A saddled riderless horse was tethered to the back. The pair of draft horses in harness snorted and shook their traces as Eliza approached, squinting up at the short heavy-set man holding the reins.

"Burrell couldn't make it, Miss," he said, seeing her confusion. "Where are the passengers? The boat's early and the captain says he won't wait."

"Which ship is it, Sir?"

"Well, it's the uh, it's the Bay City," he replied. "Hurry up, get them passengers out here!"

The flustered girl ran back to the house and flung open the front door. "The Bay City's in, Mama, and the captain won't wait!" she cried out. A moment later her mother and sisters were ushering the fugitives through the door and out to the wagon. As Jane and her daughters hurried toward the back to climb in, Mrs. Wattles suddenly exclaimed, "Why, where's Mr. Burrell?"

"Couldn't come, Ma'am," replied the driver. "He sent me in his place. Now hurry and git them folks in the wagon!"

"But who are you, Sir?" asked Esther, who knew all the abolitionists in the area. There was both command and alarm in her voice.

Suddenly, like a gunshot in the summer evening, the heavy tarpaulin covering the wagon was thrown aside. Another man Esther Wattles had never seen before, who had been kneeling beneath the canvas, stood up in the back of the wagon. He was holding a shotgun.

"Don't no one make a move!"

The driver swung down from the wagon and leveled a rifle at the stunned group of people on the ground.

"I got the mammy covered!" he announced.

Now Kirby climbed down as well. "Git in the wagon! Alla you!" he snarled, gesturing with the shotgun.

Jane looked from him to her two eldest sons. "Best do as he says," she told them in a surprisingly calm voice. "Don't do nothin' foolish. He'p me up, Alfred."

He hesitated for just a moment, his eyes burning with a dark smoldering hatred into the hard eyes of the bounty hunter.

"We can take out both you and your brother, boy," Kirby growled, "with a barrel left over for your mammy. Harness wants her dead or alive."

Jane reached for the side of the wagon to pull herself aboard before Alfred finally tore his gaze from Kirby and walked over to make a step for her with his hands.

"That's right smart of you," said Kirby. "The rest of you with her. We're gonna make us a little trip to Cleveland tonight, where the magistrate's expectin' us. Someone's bound t' be lookin' for you too," he said to the Neales. "Do like I say and nothin's gonna happen t' you or your baby."

Augustus caught Alfred's eye as their sisters followed Jane and the Neale family into the wagon. Alfred's look said as clearly as words could have that they were not going to be stopped this close to their goal. Not after all they'd been through, not when they'd finally tasted freedom, if only at a distance. But his eyes held no plan of action. *Wait, but be alert* they said. *Look for an opening.*

"You're gonna have t' git closer together than that!" yelled Kirby. "Everyone's goin' in this wagon, if you have to lay on top of each other!"

What had happened to the driver who was supposed to come for them? Where were the people at the other end, at whatever port they were to have been taken to? Maybe someone would pass them on the road tonight, word of their capture would get back to their conductor or station-master. There was no question in Alfred's mind that the two men could be overcome, but at what cost? They appeared unsurprised by the Neales. Had the family been seen and reported traveling with his own by spies somewhere along the way? With a clarity born of desperation, in the same sure manner in which he shaped and handled red-hot iron on the forge, Alfred turned their predicament over and over in his mind.

Kirby untied the trailing horse from the wagon and climbed into its saddle. How much he resembled Jeb Porter, sitting there with his shotgun in one hand and the reins in the other. Life on the Harness plantation came back to Alfred in a rush of loathing and nausea so strong it made him light-headed for a moment. But he calmed himself. Made himself think.

"Let's go, git them hosses movin'!" Kirby shouted to the driver. The wagon started off, its captive occupants making room for one another in the overcrowded bed as best they could.

Alfred was both surprised and strengthened by his mother's calm stoicism. No one could tell by the look on her face that this was anything but an annoying detour in their escape to Canada. Her refusal to admit defeat cast a spell over the wagon. Time was suspended. The fugitives appeared to be in a collective state of shock, but Alfred sensed that, though stunned, they were all just waiting. Not defeated – waiting for something to happen, someone to take command. It was up to him and Augustus to take responsibility for their family's destiny now.

Alfred knew nothing of Kirby's reputation or that the notorious bounty hunter had greedily chosen to keep most of Harness's money for himself. But he was aware of the man's contempt, for Alfred, his family, for all slaves, in hiring just a driver to help him transport the fugitives to Cleveland. This underestimation of his people would cost Kirby his reward if not his life, or it would cost Alfred his. His mother and family would not be taken back.

Kirby rode up behind the wagon. "I don't want a sound out of anyone! And like your mammy said, don't try nothin' stupid cuz it'll on'y git someone kilt. Slavery's a helluva lot better'n bein' dead ain't it?"

Alfred found Augustus's forearm in the tangle of bodies and squeezed it. *Ready, Brother*, was the response. They'd made enough of these night trips by now that both of them knew there would be interruptions along the way: branches and underbrush obstructing their passage, gullies or mud holes in the narrow dirt road, maybe even streams to cross. Any one of these could provide the distraction they'd need. Alfred's heart beat harder as he lay packed together with his family, picturing and thinking through all the obstacles they might possibly encounter. Preparing himself. Forging a ruthless determination from anxiety with an act of will. Surely this noisy wagon would arouse someone.

But an hour went by, then another. As the cold heartless stars looked on, as mile after mile the maddening insect pulse of the night enveloped the wagon, no one came between them and Cleveland.

When Alfred finally became aware of a change in the pattern of sound which seemed to have been following rather than surrounding them all night, he realized what he'd been hearing unconsciously for some time. It was water: falling or flowing rapidly over rocks, somewhere just ahead of them. Was it a stream they'd have to cross? Was there a bridge, or would they have to ford it?

Once again he squeezed Augustus's muscular forearm

and received an immediate, reassuring response. His heart began to pound and he forced himself to breathe deeply.

"Stream up ahead!" the driver called out.

"I hear it!" Kirby reined his horse to the left of the wagon and passed alongside, lowering the shotgun threateningly. "Just give me an excuse," he growled.

Jane's eldest waited only a few seconds before obliging. When Kirby reached the front of the wagon, Alfred lunged across the other passengers and leaped over the wooden side.

Would Augustus know what to do next? The lives of their whole family depended on it. It took Kirby a second or two to wheel his horse around and fire at Alfred diving into the heavy foliage beside the trail. Augustus had to grab the driver's rifle. It was their only chance.

Alfred's initial impulse had been to put the wagon between himself and Kirby, until he realized that he *had* to draw the bounty hunter's fire. His brother didn't have to think, only to react. While Kirby wasted a barrel on Alfred's retreating figure, Augustus went for the driver. His powerful legs drove him half the length of the wagon, his shoulder lowered into the man's ribs as he reached for his gun. With a groan, the driver fell backward between the wagon and horses. Only then did Augustus snatch up the rifle and take aim at Kirby. Realizing his mistake too late, the bounty hunter swung round with the shotgun to find himself dead to rights. He had sense enough to drop the gun.

"Don't shoot!" shouted Alfred, though he needn't have. Jane hadn't raised any fools. Shoot Kirby dead and even Canada wouldn't be able to protect the family. ("How long we stay alive if'n we can't keep from killin' a white man jus' 'cause he deserve it?" Augustus said later when Henry questioned his brothers' restraint.)

Alfred darted over to pick up Kirby's shotgun, then

backed safely way from him, the gun aimed squarely at his chest. He felt himself beginning to shake. "See if he has a pistol!" he yelled to Howard Neale, who like everyone else was standing in the wagon now.

"No nigger's touchin' me!" snarled Kirby.

The tension in Alfred's limbs exploded. He slammed the wooden stock of the shotgun into the side of Kirby's head, dropping him to his knees. "Just give me an excuse," he said, quivering with rage, the gun's muzzle only inches from the bounty hunter's face.

The lower half of Kirby's face had come unhinged. Putting a beefy hand tenderly to his shattered jaw, he glared at his adversary and spat blood but said no more. Howard Neale found a pistol and a derringer hidden in his filthy clothing.

Less than twenty minutes later the sound the fugitives had been desperately listening for all night proved to be the answer to their prayers. Approaching hoofbeats announced the arrival of half a dozen Lorain County abolitionists, rounded up by Robins Burrell once he'd freed himself from the ropes in which Kirby and the driver had bound him.

The bounty hunters soon found themselves on their way to Cleveland again, under escort, not at all as they had planned. While the fugitives were headed northwest to Sheffield and Lorain, where the side-wheel steamship The Mayflower was standing by for them.

21

At daybreak on a brilliant sunny day in mid-September, the Neales and Jane's family were met on the pristine shore of Lake Erie by 54-year-old Josiah Henson, who some historians believe to have been the model for Uncle Tom in Harriet Beecher Stowe's incendiary novel of slavery.

None of the fugitives had ever seen so much water. The Ohio River was wide enough to divide slave state from free, but they could see across it. This shimmering blue border extending clear to the horizon was deeply reassuring. Jane found it possible to believe that her family would indeed be safe on the other side of such a vast body of water. And tied up at the wharf was The Mayflower, the side-wheeler that was to take them to Canada.

"*Welcome*, travelers!" Henson greeted them with a big smile and outstretched arms. "You at de end of yo long journey."

Having just ventured out from under the canvas, Jane, her daughters and Rose Neale were too overwhelmed by the immense body of water before them to speak at first. Finally, Jane tore her eyes away to introduce her fellow passengers. When Henson had hugged her warmly and spoken a few words to each of her children, Jane said, "An' dis be Rose and Howard Neale. Dere chile name Freedom, cause she bo'n on de freedom trail."

"Good, *Good*!" he replied, with the same delighted

smile that had been on his face from the beginning and so much enthusiasm it had already begun to infect his passengers. "Jest 'cross Lake Erie y'all gwine be free, sho 'nough. Le's git on boa'd now. You'll see all a dat lake you wants from de boat."

Henson led them over to the wharf, where Alfred and Augustus, each taking one of Jane's arms, helped their unsteady mother up the gangplank.

"Welcome ye free souls!" the Scottish steamboat captain yelled down to them from an open window of the pilothouse. "Ye be on your way home now!"

The gangplank was quickly raised, mooring lines were cast off, and the great side-wheel sliced through the placid surface of the lake, spilling a lacy white veil over its wooden paddles. As the boat swung around into open water and a breeze washed against her face, Jane breathed a deep sigh, feeling the tears come at last. Her knees buckled but Alfred caught her.

"You all right, Mama?"

"Tired, is all. Jes he'p me over dere where's I kin rest."

The two eldest brothers helped her to a deck chair, and Jane sank into it, losing herself in this liberation of blue water before closing her eyes.

What she saw, however, wasn't Lake Erie on a beautiful September day in 1843. It was her mother Hannah as she lay dying on a pallet on the floor of her cabin, her wasted face illuminated by a single flickering candle. It was raining hard, runoff trickling and dripping through the roof in a number of places. There was no emotion in Hannah's face, only sheer exhaustion, as her eyes weakly gazed up into Jane's, who knelt on the hard dirt floor beside her mother, sobbing quietly.

The wretchedness of Hannah's existence and passing – the neat but sparsely-furnished, rickety cabin, the dirt floor, the rain coming through everywhere – tore Jane's heart as she recalled that bleak night from another time and place. She remembered her own words as if she were speaking them now for the first time: "...Dey done use you all up, Mama...did'n leave nothin. Suck you dry, lak some big evil spidah....Dey done taken yo *life*, Mama! What *right* dey have...what *right*?"

Though Hannah's face was expressionless from her immense fatigue, her wet eyes had seemed to be in complete accord with Jane's words. She tried to speak but other than a faint quivering of her lips, the effort was too great. When she died a few hours later, Jane had uttered a loud mournful wail of anguish which found release again now, on the brink of freedom for her own family: a cherished hope Hannah had never surrendered but which had eluded her in the end.

Jane's children crowded around her in alarm, but she waved them away weakly. Though deeply troubled, they honored their mother's unheard-of wish for privacy and withdrew to leave her crying silently, her sides shaking with the power of long-repressed grief.

Observing this from the pilothouse, the captain called down: "*Who'd like to come help me pilot this boat to Canada?*"

"Go on," Rachel told her younger siblings, "Car'line and I keep an eye on Mama."

Fanny and her brothers darted eagerly away to climb the stairway to the pilothouse.

"Come on in," said the captain when all three were gazing dazzled and speechless from this new vantage point at the great shoreless lake stretching before them. "This may be your only chance to pilot a steamboat. Here, young feller, take the wheel," he told Thornton. "That's right – just keep us headed straight across the lake." To the others he said, "Now then, see that man down there talking to your mother? That's Josiah Henson. He's helped more than a hundred people like yourselves escape from slavery. A good many of 'em crossed the lake on this very boat and stood right here where you're standin'."

"Right chere where *I* standin'? asked Henry.

"The very spot, sonny. Josiah Henson was a loyal slave tricked out of his freedom by a dishonest owner, so he ran away just like you folks. Then last year he started the Dawn settlement where you're headed now."

"What Dawn be like?" asked Fanny.

"It's a place where you and your family can stay long enough to find work and get an education. Then you can move on, or buy your own piece of land if you want to."

The fugitives arrived in Dawn late the next day, after spending their first night in Canada at a farm owned by free blacks who'd made much the same journey three years before. A brass bell – the same as those used on many plantations to call slaves to work – rang out, and the wagon was quickly surrounded by the community's exuberant residents.

"Welcome to Dawn, sistah!" exclaimed an elderly woman who looked to Jane about as happy as a human being could be. "We all bin hearin' 'bout yo 'scape for purt near two weeks now."

"Nevah heard of no woman an' seven chirren makin' it to Canada befo," said a hearty-looking young man Alfred's age.

"Mama, she got gumption all right," agreed Alfred, proudly supporting his exhausted mother – ain't that so, 'Gustus?"

"She de mama *an*' de man in dis fam'ly!" crowed Augustus.

"*Thank you, thank you* – we jus' so happy t' fin'ly be heah," Jane replied, clearly taken aback by the tumultuous greeting. "We could nevah done it widout de he'p of so many fine folks."

"We gwine take you to yo very own cabin now," said Henson, seeing how tired and overwhelmed she was. "An' you folks gwine share a nice big new cabin wid dese fine people from Kentucky," he told the Neales.

"How do, Rose," their new housemate greeted them. "Mah name Florence and dis here my husbin' Medford."

"How do, Ma'am. Dis be *mah* husbin' Howard –"

"An' dat be Freedom!" Medford interrupted. "We done heard all 'bout her."

While the Neales were led away to their new quarters, Josiah took Jane and her family to their modest but clean and well-built one-room cabin.

"Look, Mama!" Caroline pointed excitedly, as the door swung open to reveal a rough wood floor.

"Don' see no chinks in *dese* walls," noted Alfred.

"Look real solid-built," Augustus agreed.

"Cabins *have* to be built good up here. Ol' man winter be sumpin fierce when he gits de notion."

"Do it snow all de time?" asked Fanny.

"Not *all* de time, honey, bless yo heart," replied Henson. "It jus' seem dat way."

22

What a place Dawn be. In Guinea we be on the outside just passing through, now we live here, I still can't hardly believe we made it. Mama just like Hannah say done save her whole family. I knows when we begin to settle in that someday I'm gone get someone help me write down how it all come about, like I am now. Cabin where we live be big enough for all of us, we keeps a fire going all the time. We busy meeting and doing for people, can't keep Mama down bless her big heart but she weaker now than ever I can remember. She say don't worry about me, the Lord get my family here I be in His hands now. Baby kick now and then, I put Mama's hand where she can feel. She smile and say what she been saying ever since the night we done cross the river. Your baby be free now Caroline. Everyone make over Mama here cause of what she done but we her children gets to take care of her when she lets us.

As with Oberlin, Dawn was being built around an academic institution: the British-American Institute, founded the year before on 200 acres as a school of manual labor "for the colored inhabitants of Canada not excluding white persons and Indians." The school was intended to teach more than work skills, however, providing its students with a basic education in the ways of the world from which they had been excluded by slavery. Its founders saw Dawn as a sort of communal way station on the road to self-sufficiency for former slaves like Jane's family. The community had its own gristmill and sawmill, and its mostly black farmers raised wheat, corn, oats and tobacco on some 1,500 privately owned acres.

In their first few weeks in Dawn, as the weather grew progressively colder and more wintry, Alfred, Augustus and Thornton were kept busy cutting firewood and delivering it to some 200 residents and a constant stream of new arrivals. Being paid to work for the first time in their lives did more to drive the brothers from bed before daylight and to fuel long days of hard physical labor than either the bracing Canadian air or the hearty and plentiful food their wages helped buy.

Henry spent most of his time tagging along after Josiah Henson, in his manifold duties as Dawn's Mr. Everything: greeting newcomers and assigning them cabins and tasks; gratefully accepting donations of food, firewood and clothing from church groups and distributing them throughout the community; meeting with local Canadians seeking domestic help and farm and shop labor, as well as business enterprises or capable tradesmen in whom to risk a modest investment of idle capital; and, not least, leading church services every Sunday.

In the meantime, the distaff side of the family made the cabin more livable, gradually furnishing and decorating it with the handmade craftwork of the citizens of Dawn, from pottery to quilts to wooden implements and furniture. Life wasn't all work and worship in Dawn; when their day's tasks were over, residents went calling. Offering help was always an opportunity to socialize and make new friends, to learn more about the world from which, as slaves, they had all been sheltered so long. From the day of their arrival, as soon as their living space had been organized and made tidy, Jane and her daughters became friendly with their neighbors and began to help out where they were needed.

Despite her daughters' protests, Jane tried to do too much, both at home and in the community, and was soon spending much of her time in bed.

One night about a month after their arrival, Jane and her family attended a dance in the big rough community building constructed the year before. The interior was still being finished as carpenters and artisans in the community found the time.

From the front of the dance hall Josiah Henson looked out proudly over most of Dawn's residents, congregated in front of him in their most colorful attire. "Good t' see so many happy faces here tonight!" he said to enthusiastic response. "Befo' we commences wid de fiddlin', some folks wants to talk to you 'bout gwine back to Africa."

He gestured for two members of the American Colonization Society to come forward. The well-dressed middle-aged white men were thoroughly scrutinized as they walked to the front of the room.

"Good evening!" one of them greeted the Dawn residents, who were impatient to start the dance.

"Gettin' *cold* out there!" added the other when there was little reaction from the crowd.

"Li-*ber*-i-a!" intoned the first again. "*Liberty*! A new nation, just 20 years old, for newly free people. Think of it: a *homeland* for freed slaves. The American Colonization Society will provide freedom papers and pay passage to West Africa for all who want to go."

"*This* my homeland!" shouted a burly man about the same age as the speakers. "What I know 'bout Africa? My fam'ly been gone from Africa fo 200 years."

The second man answered him: "But isn't that where your *roots* are? Understand, we're not *asking* you to go. We're just offering you the *opportunity*."

A buxom woman in the audience called out: "All I hear is two white men tellin' me now I fin'ly free, I gots t' go back t' wheah mah ancestors dragged away from deir homes an' fam'lies an' loved ones all dose yeahs ago. Soun' lak all dis be fo *nothin'*."

"Amen, Sister!" cried several others.

"Wait a minute, brothahs an' sistahs!" shouted another member of the audience, a wiry man in his late 20s. "Dey not sayin' we *has* t' go. Dey gwine pay our way if'n we *wants* to."

"And give you your own land and seed when you get there too!" confirmed the second speaker.

"Le's get on wid de dancin'!" cried another young man, a suggestion the crowd proved to be overwhelmingly in favor of.

Josiah took his cue from the audience. "Good idee! Dese folks be 'vailable if'n you wants t' heah mo 'bout Liberia. De resta you put on dem dancin' shoes!"

The meeting broke up in excitement as Augustus and Thornton, with borrowed fiddles, joined a pianist and percussionist in front, and the large room came joyously alive. Swirling color in motion, soaring hearts, African-American music played to the brink of hysteria on the instruments of the American frontier. The more rambunctious men took turns leaving the steps of the round dance with their partners to break into their own Africanized versions of the Irish jig.

Though wrapped in warm blankets and chair-bound, Jane wouldn't have missed the dance for anything. Her smile and her lively eyes were as full of joy as any of the perspiring dancers'. She watched in satisfaction as all four of her elder children met attractive partners during the evening.

Alfred was the first to succumb to the wild abandon of the dance and the charms of the opposite sex.

"You sho has pretty eyes, missy. How long you bin heah in Dawn?"

"Long enough t' see you 'roun' de place," replied their owner, a tall slender young octoroon about Alfred's age. She was the first woman he had paid much attention to in years. Her large dark eyes seemed full of some mysterious secret, which the husky drawl in her voice was openly inviting him to try and guess. Feelings he had nearly forgotten were also bound up in those eyes, her smile, and a tone of voice that at times felt like hands along his spine.

Alfred's own smile broadened until he could feel it covering his whole face. "What yo name?"

"Ruth – laks de Bible."

"Not too familiar wid de Good Book mysel'. Couldn' let on weuns could read....Ain' you gwine ax *mah* name?"

"Oh, ah knows yo name, *Alfred*."

Still grinning guilelessly, Jane's eldest whirled Ruth around the dance floor.

Soon afterwards, in a group listening to the American Colonization Society members proselytizing on the bounties of Liberia, Rachel found herself beside the young man who had taken their side earlier.

"Dat's good of you t' speak up fo dese folks."

"Dey jus' tryin' t' be he'pful, way I sees it. No call t' treat 'em lak dey foxes nosin' roun' de henhouse....Mah name Beverly Wilson."

"*Beverly*?" said Rachel, laughing. "Dat be a girl's name!"

Unperturbed and with a sly smile he replied: "Be glad t' sho you dat ain't so."

"Ah *bets* you would," she said, lifting her eyebrows. "Kin you dance sassy as you talks?"

"You tell *me*," he said, offering Rachel his arm.

Augustus returned the fiddle to its owner later in the evening to dance with the pretty young woman who'd been eying him. At the first opportunity he introduced her to his mother.

"Mama, dis here Annie May."

"How do," said Jane. "Take someone special t git 'Gustus away from dat fiddle. Didn't have much time t' play where weuns come from."

"He do play good, don't he? Nice meetin' you, Ma'am."

Caroline, who was definitely showing by now, received her share of attention as well. A man about Alfred's age sidled over next to her and, while smiling warmly, gave her slightly swollen belly a covert glance.

"Don't have t' pretend you don't notice," she said.

"Huh? Well, ah – notice what, sistah?"

"Ah kin still dance, you know."

"Well den, le's git to it."

"Ah hopes you *moves* better'n you lies," she said as they found a place for themselves among the dancers.

Soon afterwards, Jane was helped home early by Alfred and Augustus.

"Hates t' take you 'way from dem gals."

"Dey kin wait, Mama," replied Augustus. "We wants you t' git back on yo feet again."

She gave each of them a loving look as Alfred lifted her tenderly from her chair. It shocked him how little she weighed now, but she saw nothing in her eldest son's face but his love and admiration for her. The expressions had always been there, but Jane saw how lately Alfred had become aware of the feelings himself. Here it was turning winter in a land where winter was king, and some kind of spring was taking hold in her first-born's heart.

A few days later Fanny answered a knock on the door, to find Josiah and Charlotte Henson standing in front of her family's cabin covered with snow.

"It snowin!" she exclaimed after greeting Dawn's First Couple. Dashing outside without a coat, she left it to Jane, who had broken into her nasty cough at the onrush of cold air, to invite the couple in.

"Come in, come in! Henry, put a couple a chairs by de fire. Fanny, get in here an' close dat doe!"

"Sho is good t' see dem chirren readin' like dat," said Josiah, taking note of several of Jane's children engrossed in books by fire- and candlelight as the Hensons were seated.

"Good dey has books an' be 'lowed t' read em," replied their proud mother.

"How dey learn t' read, Jane?" asked Charlotte.

"Same way *I* larn – from Mizz Harness when she reads t' her chirren. Den I gets 'em t' read t' me sometime. When my chirren small, I have 'em wid me up at de big house an' dey larns what dey can."

Josiah smiled, nodding his head appreciatively. "How you folks doin', now you been here a while?"

"Weuns doin' mighty fine, yassuh we is. We wishin' t' thankee fo dis here cabin."

"Ain't no call fo dat. Weuns come here, we had nothin' a'tall. Jest tryin' t' see you as comfitable as possible."

"Oh we be comfitable, da's fo sho –"

Jane's answer was cut short by another hacking cough.

"We hear tell they be a hard winter comin', so ah's lak if you boys kin come wid me to New Mawket in de mawnin' fo supplies."

"Sho 'nough, we kin go!" Augustus answered at once.

"Sho dey kin," affirmed Jane. "We grateful t' be of he'p."

"Gratitude be ours, Jane," Charlotte assured her.

"'Nother thing," said her husband: "we wants t' get yo chirren into school soon."

"Yassuh, be good dey larn. Dey wants to bad enough." The delighted expressions in the cabin told Henson what Jane's sons and daughters thought of the opportunity.

"Ah's gwine be lak you someday, Josiah," said Henry,

"an' he'ps folks 'scape from slav'ry lak weuns done."

Henson chuckled fondly and pulled Henry, who had been all but sitting in his lap since he and his wife sat down, onto his knee.

"Ah specks you will, Henry. Ah specks you will.... Well, we don' want to keep you folks up." He rose with his wife. "Take care a dat cough, Jane."

"Girls, make sho yo mama get her rest," said Charlotte.

"We will, Mizz Henson," promised Caroline.

"We *try*," Rachel corrected her. "Hard t' keep Mama 'way from her work."

"I know – but sometime rest mo impawtant. Remember, you *free* now!"

"...Hard t' git aholt a dat notion sometimes," said Jane, seeing the Hensons out.

She stood in the doorway behind them for a moment watching the snow fall...turning the recently cleared fields and rough-hewn buildings of Dawn into a vision of splendid and peaceful solitude. Hard to imagine that inside each silent snow-covered cabin were former slaves like herself and her seven children. All of them, every last one of them, free.

Augustus put more wood on the fire. The candles were extinguished and soon afterwards most of the family were asleep on their pallets, insulated by a thick layer of straw from the cold wooden floor. Jane lay beside her daughters under a pile of warm blankets, listening to the moaning of the wind around the corners of the cabin.

The harsh lonely sound only emphasized how protected her family was inside. She was shivering uncontrollably again; at least her cough had subsided, her children would be able to sleep soundly tonight. In her fever Jane imagined the cabin's solid log walls as an extension of her own arms, an embrace of her family, as her whole life had been. She *was* the cabin, this soft white mantle of snow, the frozen but fertile soil beneath it. And, yes, she was the river, bearing her children to freedom, the promised land.

Beneath Jane's closed lids shone a light she had never seen before. A glorious sunset. Silhouetted against it, a figure with outstretched arms awaited her. With joy flooding her heart Jane recognized her mother Hannah, smiling, smiling as only Hannah could smile. Saying to her, "You free now, girl – you *free*! You free at last!"

EPILOGUE

We all know Mama gone to leave us but I guess you never ready to lose your Mama. She buried in a real cemetery in Dawn not like on the plantation and everybody turn out to hear what nice things Josiah Henson have to say. Oh Mama its been a long long time and I still miss you.

I done have my baby girl I name Jane, she have her grammaw's spunk and fight and then some. I waits round Dawn till 1850 for James to show up knowing he ain't gone to but for my first born's sake before a freeman name of Harry Pope come to Dawn looking for his family. He about the best thing this sojourner ever see and he and little Jane hit it off too so we jump the broom then be married by Josiah Henson in church. A year later we move to Cleveland with Fanny, be here ever since.

Alfred lives in Toronto where he met a white woman name of Eleanora an Irish immigrant and done married her. We all try to guess what Mama think of that but Alfred say he know Mama love Eleanora for her high spirits if for nothing else and I believe hes right. Alfred trains horses for folks, so good at it he has horses and a stable all his own now.

Rachel done marry Beverly Wilson the man stood up for them folks full of news about Liberia soon after we arrive in Dawn. She move there with him too, none of us done seen her since but she writes she like it fine and has a family now big as mine.

Long before I move to Cleveland Augustus and Thornton got hold of some forged freedom papers and went to Oberlin where they done worked on the underground railroad while going to school. Thorntons a schoolteacher now and Augustus be a businessman with a great big fancy house we visits often as we can.

Henry stayed in Dawn the longest working alongside Josiah Henson until 1859 when he come to live with his brothers in Oberlin where he follow in their footsteps at the college. Four years we have him till he take very near the same trip we all taken to freedom only Henry done go the other way, back to Marietta where we cross the river. In 1863 he done join the 27th Colored Infantry Regiment of the Union Army, killed God rest his soul a year later in what be called the Battle of Cold Harbor in Petersburg, Virginia. Alfred say Henry never should have crossed back over that river but I say somehow he following in Mama's footsteps. We always did call him Mama's shadow.

If you liked Jane's story pass it on!

If you were moved by this mother's courage and the determination by others, regardless of the consequences, to free her family, tell your friends. Call the editor of your newspaper, the principal of your child's school, your librarian. Ask your local bookstore to make *The River Jordan* available in your community.

Remember, too, that you can order books directly from the publisher by calling the toll-free number: **(800) 239-6229**.

If you believe, as we do, that Jane's true story has much to teach our children and people young and old alike, of every race and nationality...be a messenger. The spirit of the Underground Railroad – the courage, compassion and humanity that saved thousands of lives from slavery – were never needed more than they are today.

Fifteen percent of the authors' royalties from the sale of *The River Jordan* will go to the Escape-of-Jane Foundation to support the study and commemoration of the Underground Railroad, an American institution which can *still* bring inspiration to people around the world.

SELECTED BIBLIOGRAPHY

Brandt, Nat. *The Town That Started the Civil War*. Syracuse University Press, 1990

Franklin, John Hope, and Schweninger, Loren. *Runaway Slaves;Rebels on the Plantation*. Oxford University Press, 1999

Hardesty's Pleasants County, H.H. Hardesty & Co. *West Virginia Heritage Encyclopedia*. Edited and compiled by Jim Comstock, 1974

Jacobs, Harriet A. *Incidents in the Life of a Slave Girl*. Harvard University Press, 1987

Kemble, Frances Anne. *Journal of a Residence on a Georgian Plantation in 1838-1839*. University of Georgia Press, 1984

Siebert, Wilbur H. *The Mysteries of Ohio's Underground Railroads*. Long's College Book Co., 1951

Stowe, Harriet Beecher. *Uncle Tom's Cabin, or, Life Among The Lowly*. John P. Jewett and Co., 1853

Swick, Ray. *An Island Called Eden*, 1995

Winks, Robin W. *The Blacks in Canada*. McGill-Queen's University Press, 1997

Zimmer, Louise. *True Stories of Pioneer Times*, 1987

Zimmer, Louise. *More True Stories from Pioneer Valley*. Sugden Book Store, 1993

Co-authors Henry Burke (l), and Dick Croy